DK EYEWITNESS TRAVEL

TOP 10 BEIJING

ANDREW HUMPHREYS

Penguin Random House

Top 10 Beijing Highlights

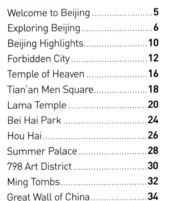

The Top 10 of Everything

CONTENTS

Beijing Area by Area

Streetsmart

Within each Top 10 list in this book, no hierarchy of quality or popularity is implied. All 10 are, in the editor's opinion, of roughly equal merit.

Throughout this book, floors are referred to in accordance with American usage; i.e., the "first floor" is at ground level.

Front cover and spine *The Temple of Heaven*
Back cover *Beijing's financial district*
Title page *The Nine Dragon Screen at Bei Hai Park*

The information in this DK Eyewitness Top 10 Travel Guide is checked regularly. Every effort has been made to ensure that this book is as up-to-date as possible at the time of going to press. Some details, however, such as telephone numbers, opening hours, prices, gallery hanging arrangements and travel information, are liable to change. The publishers cannot accept responsibility for any consequences arising from the use of this book, nor for any material on third party websites, and cannot guarantee that any website address in this book will be a suitable source of travel information. We value the views and suggestions of our readers very highly. Please write to: Publisher, DK Eyewitness Travel Guides, Dorling Kindersley, 80 Strand, London WC2R 0RL, Great Britain, or email travelguides@dk.com

Welcome to
Beijing

From ornate temples and palaces to hip cafés and bars, Beijing's many attractions make it a great place to explore. In just three decades, China's capital has transformed itself from a socialist monolith to a cosmopolitan metropolis, with all the arts, culture, entertainment, and glamor that entails. With Eyewitness Top 10 Beijing, the city is at your fingertips.

Less than 15 years ago, the residents of downtown Beijing were cycling around in their pyjamas, and mules pulling carts of bricks through the streets were a common sight. But over the last decade, the city has experienced an incredible rate of growth. Today, Beijing is dotted with Olympic sites such as the **Bird's Nest** and the **Water Cube**, state-of-the-art venues including the **National Center for the Performing Arts,** and edgy art districts like **798** and **Caochangdi**, while Sanlitun is filled with chic boutiques.

Yet amid this cosmopolitan city, lovers of antiquities still have plenty to see. The **Forbidden City** anchors the capital, and the **Summer Palace** offers respite from city noise. The conical **Temple of Heaven** graces countless guidebooks, and there are houses of worship on almost every corner – from Taoist (**White Cloud Temple**) to Buddhist (**Lama and Fayuan**) and Confucian to Catholic. However, the city's real charm lies in its *hutongs* – 800-year-old warrens that wind through the center – and a walk around **Hou Hai** lake, with its historical courtyard houses, offers a further glimpse of everyday life in Beijing.

Whether you're coming for a weekend or a week, our Top 10 Guide brings together the best of Beijing, from temple fairs to traditional crafts and tea. The guide also offers handy tips throughout, revealing the best free things to do in the city and how to avoid the crowds, as well as eight easy-to-follow itineraries designed to help you visit a clutch of sights in a short space of time. Add inspiring photography and detailed maps, and you've got the perfect pocket-sized companion. **Enjoy the book, and enjoy Beijing.**

Clockwise from top: **Great Wall of China, Temple of Heaven, the Forbidden City, Beijing's financial district, painting at the Ming Tombs, the National Stadium, Chinese lanterns**

Exploring Beijing

Beijing combines ancient history with accelerated progress, but information can be sketchy and transportation difficult, even for Chinese speakers. These two itineraries include the city's highlights and offer advice on how to make the most of your time.

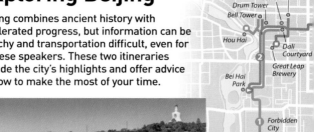

Bei Hai Park is a former imperial garden. Its lake is popular for boating.

Two Days in Beijing

Day ❶
MORNING
Do some morning tai chi with the locals at the **Temple of Heaven** (see pp16–17), then browse the art stores on **Liulichang** (see p78). Stop for roast duck at **Deyuan** (see p79), then head into **Tian'an Men Square** (see pp18–19) and the **Forbidden City** (see pp12–15).
AFTERNOON
Leave by the north gate and walk to **Bei Hai Park** (see pp24–5), then over to the **Drum and Bell Towers** (see p26) for a rickshaw ride around the *hutongs* (traditional lanes). Enjoy a Yunnan dinner at **Dali Courtyard** (see p85), then grab a sundowner in **Hou Hai** (see pp26–7) – but BYOB.

Day ❷
MORNING
Hire a car for a trip to the **Great Wall** (see pp34–5), and make your way to Mutianyu. After hiking, grab some country-style lunch at a local spot.
AFTERNOON
Visit the **Summer Palace** (see pp28–9). Relax in the Garden of Virtue and Harmony, or go boating on Kunming Lake. End the day with dinner on **Gui Jie** (Ghost Street) (see p90).

Four Days in Beijing

Day ❶
MORNING
Start off with the **Forbidden City** (see pp12–15), then wander through **Tian'an Men Square** (see pp18–19). For lunch, head south into the *hutongs* to find **Southern Fish** (see p79).
AFTERNOON
Visit the **Temple of Heaven** (see pp16–17), then stroll over to **Dazhalan** (Dashilan) (see p75) for some window shopping, grabbing a coffee at **Spoonful of Sugar** (see p79). Circle back to Qian Men for dinner and drinks at **Capital M** (see p79), with the best view in the city.

Day ❷
MORNING
Join the locals in **Bei Hai Park** (see pp24–5) for some morning tai chi

The Great Wall at Mutianyu dates from the 14th century.

Yunnan food on the terrace at **Yun'er** (see p85), then wander down bustling Nanluoguxiang for some craft beer at the **Great Leap Brewery** (see p84).

Day ③
MORNING
Get an early start and hire a private car to take you to the **Summer Palace** (see pp28–9). Stop at the **Ming Tombs** (see pp32–3), then go on to the **Great Wall** (see pp34–5). Enjoy a late countryside lunch at Mutianyu.
AFTERNOON
Hike to your heart's content, then sleep on a *kang* (traditional bed) in a farmer's house after a rustic dinner.

Day ④
MORNING
Leave after breakfast and head back to the city, stopping at the **798 Art District** (see pp30–31).
AFTERNOON
Grab some lunch at **AT Café** (see p31), and check out some of the galleries that have made Chinese art famous. Head back downtown to Sanlitun for roast duck at **Jing Yaa Tang** (see p93), then take a wander over to **Migas** (see p93) for alfresco after-dinner drinks.

Key
— Two day itinerary
— Four day itinerary

and water calligraphy, then wander over toward the **Drum and Bell Towers** in Hou Hai (see pp26–7). Get lost in the *hutongs* and stop at **Mr Shi's Dumplings** (see p57) for lunch.
AFTERNOON
Continue down leafy Guozijian Street. Check out the traditional craft shops and **Confucius Temple** (see p82) before heading to the **Lama Temple** (see pp20–21). Dine on excellent

The Hall of Prayer for Good Harvests can be found at **The Temple of Heaven**.

Top 10 Beijing Highlights

Colorful pavilion atop the
Forbidden City's North Gate

🔟 Beijing Highlights

At the heart of Beijing is tradition, symbolized by the Forbidden City, home to successive imperial dynasties for five centuries. Nearby, Tian'an Men Square is the China of recent times, of socialism and Mao. Beijing is also a city on the move, as a spirit of change makes it the most 21st century of capitals.

Forbidden City ①

So called because at one time only members of the imperial court were allowed inside, this is one of the largest and greatest palace complexes ever built *(see pp12–15)*.

② Temple of Heaven

Originally the venue for annual winter solstice sacrifices, which were performed by successive emperors to ensure ample harvests, the temple remains Beijing's most recognizable icon *(see pp16–17)*.

Tian'an Men Square ③

The world's largest public square is not pretty, but it is surrounded by august cultural and political institutions, and it is also the final resting place of Chairman Mao Zedong *(see pp18–19)*.

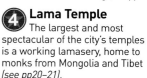

④ Lama Temple

The largest and most spectacular of the city's temples is a working lamasery, home to monks from Mongolia and Tibet *(see pp20–21)*.

⑤ Bei Hai Park

The most beautiful of Beijing's many city parks is laid out around a central lake, first dug out in the 12th century, with the excavated earth used to create a central island. The famed Kublai Khan ruled his empire from a palace here *(see pp24–5)*.

TIUGLOULOU DAJIE
GUOWAN HUTON
⑥
Qian Hai
DIAN MEN WAI DAJIE
DIAN MEN XI DAJIE
⑤
Bei Hai
DIAN MEN
Jing Shan Park
WENJIN JIE
JING SHAN QIAN JIE
Zhong Hai
NANCHANG JIE
①
Nan Hai
XI CHANG'AN JIE
③
QIAN MEN XI DAJIE
QIAN MEN DAJIE
TIANQIAO NAN DAJIE
ZHUSHIKOU XI DAJIE

6 Hou Hai

By day visitors take rickshaw tours around the back lanes for a glimpse of fast-disappearing old Beijing; by night, attention shifts to the area's lakeside bars and restaurants *(see pp26–7)*.

Around Beijing 10
Great Wall of China
S398 S325 HUAIROU
S398 G45
9 Ming Tombs S330
CHANGPING
SHUNYI
S550 G45
Summer Palace S550 7 8 798 Art District
SHIJINGSHAN TONGZHOU
Area of main map
0 km 15
0 miles 15

0 kilometers 1
0 miles 1

CHONGWEN

Tian Tan Park 2

7 Summer Palace

Beijing summers are unbearably hot, so the imperial court would exchange the Forbidden City for this semi-rural retreat, with its ornate pavilions and gardens, ranged around Kunming Lake *(see pp28–9)*.

8 798 Art District

When former electronic components factory 798 became a venue for contemporary art, it kick-started a local trend for converting industrial spaces into galleries and chic bars *(see pp30–31)*.

9 Ming Tombs

Thirty miles (45 km) northwest of Beijing is the vast burial site of 13 of China's 16 Ming emperors. The most impressive sight here is the Sacred Way, with its 12 pairs of stone guardians *(see pp32–3)*.

10 Great Wall of China

"Great" is something of an understatement; the Wall is nothing less than spectacular. Clamber up the perilously sloping carriageways to one of the highest watchtowers on the wall – the experience is breathtaking *(see pp34–5)*.

🔟⭐ Forbidden City

Officially known as the Palace Museum, this magnificent complex is a grand monument to the 24 emperors who ruled from its halls over a period of almost 500 years. The symbolic center of the Chinese universe, the palace was the exclusive domain of the imperial court from its completion in 1420 until the last of the emperors was forced to abdicate at the beginning of the 20th century. The modern world intruded in 1949, when the public were finally admitted through the palace gates. A limit of 80,000 visitors per day remains in force.

Meridian Gate ①
Known in Chinese as the *Wu Men*, this gate is the traditional entrance to the palaces. From the balcony **(right)** the emperor would review his armies and perform ceremonies marking the start of the new lunar year.

② Hall of Supreme Harmony
Raised on a triple tier of marble terraces, this largest of halls houses a sandalwood throne **(left)**, used in the coronations of 24 emperors.

③ Inner Court
The Inner Court is more intimate than the formal Outer Court, because this is where the emperor and empress lived, close to the emperor's concubines.

NEED TO KNOW
MAP L3 ■ North of Tian'an Men Square ■ 8500 7420 ■ Subway: Tian'an Men West or Tian'an Men East ■ www.dpm.org.cn

Open Apr–May & Sep–Oct: 8:30am–5pm Tue–Sun; Jun–Aug: 8:30am–5pm daily; Nov–Mar: 8:30am–4:30pm Tue–Sun

Adm Apr–Oct ¥60; Nov–Mar ¥40; there are additional charges for certain halls; audio guides are available for ¥40 (plus ¥100 deposit)

■ There are snack kiosks near the ticket office, and a restaurant inside.

■ Enter through the Meridian Gate only; other gates are for exit.

④ Imperial Garden
The emperor Qianlong wrote, "Every ruler [...] must have a garden in which he can stroll, and relax his heart." This formal garden, the oldest in the Forbidden City, has two beautiful pavilions **(below)**.

7 Hall of Preserving Harmony

The most spectacular aspect of this hall **(left)** is the great carved ramp on the north side, sculpted with dragons and clouds, and made from a single piece of marble weighing more than 200 tons.

THE LAST EMPEROR

Pu Yi rose to power aged three in 1908, but he was forced to abdicate in 1912 by the new Republican government. The ex-emperor continued to live in the Forbidden City until 1924. He was later imprisoned by the Communists, until Mao granted him amnesty in 1959. He died in 1967, after working for seven years as a gardener.

Forbidden City

10 Gate of Supreme Harmony

The fourth and final great gate gives access to the Outer Court, the heart of the Forbidden City. The gate is guarded by two large bronze lions, classic imperial symbols of power and dignity.

5 Eastern Palaces

East of the Inner Court are smaller halls. This is where the emperor's harem once lived.

6 Western Palaces

It took a decade to restore the Western Palaces, with six now open to the public. These include the Palace of Gathered Elegance and the Palace of Eternal Spring, both associated with the Empress Dowager Cixi *(see p29)*.

8 Gate of Heavenly Purity

The oldest hall of all is the boundary between the Outer Court (official) and Inner Court (private).

9 Golden Water

Five bridges span the Golden Water **(below)**, which flows from west to east in a course designed to resemble the jade belt worn by the court officials.

🔟 Forbidden City Collections

1 Ceramics
Several halls around the Inner Court display tomb figurines from the Sui (581–618) and Tang (618–906) dynasties. Statues range from six inches to three feet (15 cm to 1 m) in height, and depict overweight court ladies, Buddhas on elephants, and floppy-humped camels. A film offers some background on the pottery finds.

Delicately decorated ceramic vase

2 Scientific Instruments
Enlightened Qing emperor Kangxi (1654–1722) appointed Europeans as court officials, and instructed his imperial workshops to re-create Western scientific instruments. These included astro-nomical tools, calculators, sundials, and a table with measurements and scientific notations. The instruments are part of the Imperial Treasures of the Ming and Qing dynasties exhibit, on the west side of the Inner Court.

3 Jade
The Hall of Quintessence was once where dowager empresses went to die; it now exhibits jade artifacts. Pieces range from simple cups and ladles to enormous and intricate sculptures of Buddhas in traditional settings. The Chinese considered working this hard stone to be a metaphor for character development and the pursuit of perfection.

4 Jewelry
In the Hall of Moral Cultivation are three of the six halls of "jewelry" (head north for rooms four through six), including the only hall to display traditional jewelry rather than agate cups or jade sculpture. Hall number three has thick jade rings, lapis lazuli court beads, elaborate headdresses made of gold filigree phoenixes, and even jadeite Christian rosary beads.

5 Beijing Opera
The Pavilion of Cheerful Melodies sports a three-story stage able to accommodate 1,000 actors. It was once rigged with trapdoors and pulleys to create dramatic entrances for supernatural characters. The exhibits include a behind-the-scenes model stage, as well as costumes, instruments, scripts, and cast lists. Screens show reconstructions of old court performances.

Dramatic scene unfolding on stage during a Beijing Opera performance

6 Musical Instruments

In true imperial fashion, the more lavish the musical entertainment, the more glory it reflected on the emperor. Court musicians used gongs of all sizes and *guqins* (zithers), wooden flutes, and heavy bronze bells adorned with dragons, as well as the unusual *sheng*, a Sherlock Holmes-style pipe with reeds of different lengths sprouting from the top. The collection is displayed in the Silver Vault of the Imperial Palace, on the west side of the Outer Court.

Pagoda-topped four-sided clock

embroidered red silk decorated with ornate Chinese mythological symbols.

9 Clocks and Watches

Arguably the finest of the many palace collections, the clocks and watches fill the Fengxian Pavilion in the southeastern corner of the eastern Inner Court. The creativity involved in some of the pieces – which are primarily European – is astonishing. One particularly inventive model has an automaton clad in European dress frantically writing eight Chinese characters on a scroll, which is being unrolled by two other mechanical figures.

Bells in the instrument collection

7 Stone Drums

The Hall of Moral Cultivation holds the palace's collection of stone drums. These are enormous tom-tom shaped rocks that bear China's earliest stone inscriptions, dating back to 374 BC. These ideographic carvings are arranged in four-character poems, which commemorate the glorious pasture-land and successful animal husbandry made possible by the Emperor Xiangong's benevolence.

8 Daily Life of the Concubines

Every three years, court officials would select girls between the ages of 13 and 17 to join the eight ranks of imperial concubines. The Yonghe Pavilion exhibits clothing, games, herbal medicine, and a food distribution chart relating to the young imperial consorts, as well as the "wedding night bed," which is covered in a richly

10 Empress Cixi

The Xianfu Pavilion is a memorial to the Empress Cixi's devious rise to power *(see p29)*, as well as to the great lady's imperial extravagances, which so nearly crippled her country. Clothes, jewelry, embroidered socks, imported perfume, jade and ivory chopsticks, and pictures of clothes and food form the bulk of the exhibits. There are also examples of the empress's calligraphic skills in the form of painted wall hangings.

Empress Cixi's display, Xianfu Pavilion

TOP 10 ★ Temple of Heaven (Tian Tan)

As the Son of Heaven, the emperor could intercede with the gods on behalf of his people. It was here that he would pray at the winter solstice for a good harvest. Off-limits to the common people during the Ming and Qing dynasties, the complex is now open to the public and attracts thousands of visitors daily, including many locals who come to enjoy the huge park in which the temple is set.

1 Hall of Prayer for Good Harvests

Built in 1420, then rebuilt in 1889, this circular tower, with a conical roof of blue tiles and a gold finial, is the most beautiful building in Beijing. One of the most striking facts about it is that it was constructed without the use of a single nail.

2 Painted Caisson Ceiling

The circular ceiling of the Hall of Prayer for Good Harvests has a gilded dragon and phoenix at its center **(below)**. The wood for the four central columns was imported from Oregon, as at the time China had no trees tall enough.

3 Temple of Heaven Park

Today, locals, inured to both the splendor of the buildings and the crowds of tourists, use the vast grounds to practice tai chi and to exercise.

4 Imperial Vault of Heaven

A circular hall made of wood and capped by a conical roof, the Imperial Vault **(above)** once held the wooden spirit tablets that were used in the ceremonies that took place on the nearby Round Altar.

5 Round Altar

The altar is formed of marble slabs laid out in nine concentric circles with each gray circle containing a multiple of nine pieces. The center of the altar represents the center of the world and it is where the emperor carried out sacrifices.

6 Echo Stones

There are three rectangular stones at the foot of the staircase leading up to the Imperial Vault: stand on the first and clap to hear one echo; stand on the second stone and clap once for two echoes; clap once on the third for three echoes.

Temple of Heaven (Tian Tan)

TIAN TAN

The Hall of Prayer for Good Harvests, or Qinian Dian, which is the iconic structure at the heart of the complex, is often incorrectly called the Temple of Heaven. There is, in fact, no single temple building and the name, which in Chinese is Tian Tan – a more literal translation of which is Altar of Heaven – refers to the whole complex.

8 Marble Platform

The Hall of Prayer for Good Harvests sits atop three tiers of marble that form a circle 300 ft (90 m) in diameter **(right)**. The balusters on the upper tier are decorated with dragon carvings that signify the imperial nature of the structure.

9 Red Step Bridge

A raised walkway of marble and stone that runs along the north-south axis of the complex, the Red Step Bridge **(below)** connects the Hall of Prayer for Good Harvests with the Round Altar.

7 Echo Wall

The Imperial Vault is enclosed by the circular Echo Wall, which has the same sonic effects found in some European cathedrals, where even a whisper travels round to a listener on the other side.

NEED TO KNOW

MAP F6 ■ Tian Tan Dong Lu (East Gate), Chongwen ■ 6702 8866 ■ Subway: Tian Tan Dong Men ■ www.tiantanpark.com

Open Park: 6am–10pm daily. Temple: 8am–5:30pm daily (Jul–Oct: to 6pm daily; Nov–Feb: to 5pm daily)

Adm ¥35 (to temple), ¥15 (to park), audio guides ¥40, plus deposit of ¥100

■ There are snack kiosks in the park grounds.

■ Just as fascinating as exploring the temple is observing the many Chinese who come to the park to dance, exercise, sing opera, and fly kites.

10 Hall of Abstinence

A red-walled compound surrounded by a moat spanned by bridges, this hall resembles a mini Forbidden City. This is where the emperor would spend the last 24 hours of his three-day fast prior to partaking in the Temple of Heaven ceremonies.

🔟 ⭐ Tian'an Men Square

Tian'an Men Guangchang (Square of the Gate of Heavenly Peace) is not the world's most attractive public plaza. It also has unfortunate associations with death, in the shape of Mao's Mausoleum and in the memories of the bloody climax of 1989's pro-democracy rallies. However, it is central to modern life in Beijing, surrounded by major national institutions, and filled daily with visitors and kite flyers.

① National Museum of China

This 1959 building on the eastern side of the square combines the Museum of Chinese History and the Museum of the Revolution. Forty-eight galleries show Chinese history, art, and archaeology exhibits **(below)**.

④ Tian'an Men

On October 1, 1949, Mao proclaimed the founding of the People's Republic of China from this massive Ming-dynasty gate **(right)**, where his huge portrait is still prominently displayed. The way to the Forbidden City is through here.

② Great Hall of the People

A monolithic structure dominating the western side of the square, the Great Hall is the seat of the Chinese legislature. The vast auditorium and banqueting halls are open for part of every day except when the People's Congress is in session.

⑤ Arrow Tower

Along with the Qian Men, the Arrow Gate formed part of a great double gate. The walls that once flanked the gate were eventually demolished in the 20th century.

⑥ Railway Museum

Built by the British in 1906, China's first ever passenger train station now houses a Railway Museum. Perfect for train enthusiasts, old photos, model trains, and a full-sized replica of a modern high-speed train driver's cabin are on display.

③ Qian Men

Also known as Zhengyang Men ("Sun-facing Gate"), the "Front Gate" **(right)** was built during the Ming dynasty. It was the largest of the nine gates of the inner city wall. It now houses a city history museum.

7 National Flag

The Chinese flag flies at the northern end of Tian'an Men Square. People's Liberation Army (PLA) soldiers raise the flag each day at dawn and lower it back down again as the sun begins to set over the city.

9 Bicycles

While there are allegedly 10 million bikes registered in Beijing, every day as many as 1,300 new cars are added to the city's congested roads. Smog levels in the city are a serious problem.

CITY WALLS

It was during the Ming era (1368–1644) that the walls took on their recognizable shape of an outer wall with seven gates, and an inner wall with nine gates. Rather tragically, almost all was demolished in the 1950s and 1960s, although a small portion still stands south of Beijing Station. Today the gates are remembered in the names of the subway stations situated on the Second Ring Road.

Tian'an Men Square

8 Mao's Mausoleum

In an imposing hall at the center of Tian'an Men Square lies the embalmed body of Mao Zedong, who died in 1976. Encased in a crystal casket and draped in a red flag, the founding father of Communist China is raised from his refrigerated chamber for daily public viewings.

NEED TO KNOW

MAP L5 ■ Subway: Tian'an Men West, Tian'an Men East, or Qian Men

National Museum of China: 6511 6400; open 9am–5pm Tue–Sun (Jul & Aug: 8am–6pm Tue–Sun); free with valid ID

Mao's Mausoleum: 6513 2277; open 8am–noon Tue–Sun; free with valid ID; taking in handbags, backpacks, cameras, food, and drinks is prohibited

Qian Men: 6522 9384; open 8:30am–4pm daily; adm ¥20

Railway Museum: 6705 1638; open 9am–5pm Tue–Sun; adm ¥20

Tian'an Men: 6524 3322; open 8:30am–4:30pm daily; adm ¥15

■ Entry to Tian'an Men Square comes with thorough security checks, so schedule plenty of time for lines.

10 Monument to the Heroes

Erected in 1958, the granite monument (below) is decorated with bas-reliefs from episodes from the nation's revolutionary history and calligraphy from Communist veterans Mao Zedong and Zhou Enlai.

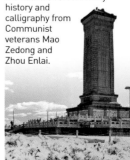

⑩ ⭐ Lama Temple (Yonghe Gong)

Beijing's most spectacular place of worship is also the most famous Buddhist temple outside of Tibet. It has five main halls, as well as some stunning statuary. The path through the Lama Temple proceeds from south to north – from earth to heaven.

① Hall of the Heavenly Kings

The first hall has a plump laughing Buddha, Milefo, back-to-back with Wei Tuo, the Guardian of Buddhist Doctrine. They are flanked by the Four Heavenly Kings.

② Hall of Eternal Harmony

This, the second hall, contains three manifestations of Buddha **(right)** representing the past, present, and future. They are flanked by 18 *luohan* – those freed from the cycle of rebirth.

③ Hall of Eternal Protection

The third hall **(below)** contains Buddhas of longevity and medicine, plus two *tangkas* said to have been embroidered by Emperor Qianlong's mother. Behind the hall is a bronze sculpture of Mount Meru.

④ Hall of the Wheel of Dharma

Hall four has a large statue of Tsongkhapa, the 14th-century founder of the Yellow Hat sect of Buddhism. Dominant in Tibetan politics for centuries, the sect is led by the Dalai Lama and Panchen Lama.

⑤ Monks

At one time there were 1,500 monks at the temple; now there are only around 70. Although of the same Yellow Hat sect as the Dalai Lama, the monks are required to reject Tibetan independence.

⑥ Hall of Ten Thousand Happinesses

The final pavilion houses an 80-ft (25-m) high Buddha carved from a single piece of sandalwood. There's a splendid collection of Tibetan Buddhist objects in a room behind the hall.

⑦ Prayer Wheel

Spinning a prayer wheel sends a prayer written on coiled paper to heaven. A little yellow arrow taped to the frame of the wheel reminds worshipers which direction (clockwise) to spin the wheel.

8 Lion Statue

A large imperial lion **(left)** is a reminder that the complex was the residence of future Qing emperor Yongzheng. On ascending the throne in 1722, and in keeping with tradition, his former home became a temple.

PANCHEN LAMA

While the Dalai Lama, head of the sect to which the Lama Temple belongs, lives in exile, the second head, the Panchen Lama, resides in Beijing. In contrast to the Dalai Lama, the Panchen recognizes Chinese authority. However, the matter of the true identity of the Panchen Lama is mired in controversy. China supports one candidate, while the Tibetans recognize another – only he vanished in suspicious circumstances in 1995.

Lama Temple (Yonghe Gong)

9 Incense Burner

There are incense burners **(below)** in front of all the many altars throughout the temple. Shops lining the entryway to the complex and in the neighboring streets are piled with bundles of incense sticks for sale for use at the temple.

10 Drum and Bell Towers

The temple's Drum and Bell towers are in the first courtyard after passing through the main entrance. The huge bell has been removed from its tower and placed on the ground **(above)**.

NEED TO KNOW

MAP F1 ■ 12 Yonghe Gong Dajie ■ 6404 4499 ■ Subway: Yonghe Gong ■ www.yonghegong.cn

Open 9am–4.30pm daily (Nov–Mar: to 4pm)

Adm ¥25, audio guides ¥20 (plus ¥200 deposit)

■ There are various snack kiosks inside the Lama Temple, but it is a better idea to bring your own refreshments.

■ Photography is not allowed within the halls, but you can take pictures of the exteriors and of the courtyards.

Following pages The blue-tiled Hall of Prayer for Good Harvests, Temple of Heaven

TOP 10 ⭐ Bei Hai Park

An imperial garden for over 1,000 years, Bei Hai was opened to the public in 1925. Filled with artificial hills, pavilions, and temples, it is associated with Kublai Khan, who redesigned it during the Mongol Yuan dynasty. These days, it is a fine place for a leisurely stroll, and a bit of boating on the lake.

1 Round City
Bei Hai was the site of Beijing's earliest imperial palace, although nothing now remains other than a small pavilion on a site known as the Round City, and a large jade wine vessel said to have belonged to Kublai Khan.

2 The Place of Serenity
In the northwest corner of the park is this utterly beautiful garden, created in the mid-18th century by the Qianlong emperor, with rockeries, pavilions, and ornate bridges over goldfish-filled pools.

3 Three Temples
Near the Place of Serenity is a trio of small temple buildings – the Pavilion of 10,000 Buddhas **(left)**, the Glazed Pavilion, which is covered with green and yellow ceramic Buddhas, and the Xiao Xitian (Small Western Sky) Temple filled with fearsome-looking idols.

4 White Dagoba
Topping Jade Island, this is a Tibetan-style stupa built to honor the visit of the fifth Dalai Lama in 1651. It has been rebuilt twice since.

PARK PLAY
Beijing's parks double as recreation centers, particularly for the city's elderly citizens. Early in the morning, they gather to perform *tai ji quan* (tai chi) exercises. Many then spend the rest of the day in the park playing cards or mahjong, engaging in *yang ge* (fan dancing) or ballroom dancing, or just reading the paper and talking with friends.

5 Jade Island
Accessed by bridge from the south gate or by boat from the north gate, Bei Hai's willow-lined island **(below)** was created from the earth excavated to form the lake.

9 Yongan Temple
Located beneath the Dagoba on Jade Island, this temple comprises a series of ascending halls, including the Hall of the Wheel of Law, with its central effigy of the Buddha Sakyamuni **(left)**.

7 Pavilion of Calligraphy
A crescent-shaped hall on Jade Island contains nearly 500 stone tablets engraved with the work of famous Chinese calligraphers. If the exhibits are less than enthralling, the walkways that lead to the pavilion are enchanting.

8 Zhong Nan Hai
Bei Hai means "North Lake"; the Middle (Zhong) and South (Nan) Lakes are part of an area occupied by China's political leaders and are off-limits to all except government officials. Zhong Nan Hai is regarded as the new Forbidden City.

10 Fangshan Restaurant
Founded in 1926 by chefs of the imperial household, the restaurant **(above)** bases its menus on court cuisine. Standards have slipped, but the opulent setting still has great appeal.

6 Nine Dragon Screen
This free-standing wall made of colorful glazed ceramic tiles depicts nine intertwined dragons **(above)**. The Chinese dragon is a beneficent beast offering protection and good luck. The wall was designed to obstruct the passage of evil spirits.

NEED TO KNOW

MAP K1 ■ 1 Wenjin Jie, Xicheng ■ 6403 3225 ■ info@beihaipark.com.cn ■ Subway: Tian'an Men West ■ Buses: 5, 101, 103, 107, 109, 111, and others

Open Apr–Oct: 6:30am–9pm daily; Nov–Mar: 6:30am–8pm. Buildings close 5pm Apr–Oct, 4pm Nov–Mar

Adm Apr–Oct ¥10, Nov–Mar ¥5

■ There are snack kiosks in the park.

■ There are four gates to the park: the most convenient is the south gate, close to the Forbidden City; the north gate exits across the road from Hou Hai, where there are good eating and drinking options.

🔟 ⭐ Hou Hai

The area around the joined lakes of Qian Hai and Hou Hai has traditionally been home to nobles and wealthy merchants. Several grand homes survive, hidden in the labyrinthine old lanes known as *hutongs*. This is a rare quarter of Beijing where the 21st century is kept at bay, and these back alleys represent one of the most satisfying parts of the city to explore on foot – or by rickshaw.

① Boating and skating
In summer the lakes are filled with small pedal boats. By mid-December, they are frozen over **(below)** and a large area is cordoned off for ice-skating.

② Silver Ingot Bridge
The narrow channel that connects Hou Hai's two lakes is spanned by the pretty, arched Silver Ingot Bridge, which dates from the time of the Yuan dynasty (1279–1368).

③ Former Residence of Guo Moruo
Beijing's many "former residences of" are mostly connected with Party favorites. Moruo was an author and key figure in the rise of Communism in China.

④ Hutongs
The lakes **(above)** lie at the heart of a sprawling old district, characterized by traditional alleyways known as *hutongs*. These alleys are lined for the most part by the blank outer walls of *siheyuan*, which are inward-looking houses arranged around a central courtyard.

⑤ Drum and Bell Towers
Just north of the eastern end of Yandai Xie Jie, these two imposing towers once marked the northernmost limits of the city. You can ascend the towers for views of Hou Hai and beyond.

NEED TO KNOW

MAP D2 ■ Subway: Shicha Hai, Jishuitan

Mansion of Prince Gong: 8328 8149; open Apr–Oct: 8am–5pm daily; Nov–Mar: 9am–4pm daily; adm ¥40 or ¥70 with tour guide, tea and snack tasting, and traditional opera performance (call ahead for times); www.pgm.org.cn

Former Residence of Guo Moruo: 6612 5984; open 9am–4.30pm Tue–Sun; closed Dec 25 until 5th day of Chinese New Year; adm ¥20

Song Qingling's Residence: 6404 4205; open 9am–4:30pm Tue–Sun; admission ¥20

■ Visit Hou Hai by day to explore the *hutongs* and historic residences, but come back later to dine and see the lake glimmering with the flotilla of tea-candles that are floated out on the water each evening.

■ The Hou Hai area has several excellent restaurants and bars *(see pp84–5)*.

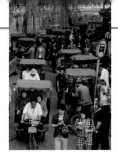

8 Rickshaw tours

One way of seeing the *hutongs* is from a rickshaw **(left)**. Prices are negotiable, but expect to pay around ¥180 per person for a two-hour jaunt with the occasional stop-off.

Hou Hai

10 Mansion of Prince Gong

This former residence of Prince Gong is a preserved historic mansion in Beijing. The garden is a pattern of corridors and pavilions, dotted with pools and gates **(below)**.

6 Song Qingling's Residence

Song Qingling was the wife of the revolutionary leader Sun Yat Sen. Her former living quarters are now a small museum. The gardens surrounding the house are beautiful.

9 Yandai Xie Jie

One of the busiest tourist streets in Beijing, Yandai Xie Jie is lined with historic buildings, most of which have been converted into small boutiques and bars, including a temple that is now a café.

7 Lotus Lane

This is Hou Hai's main lakeside parade of restaurants, bars, and cafés **(below)**. Many of these establishments boast attractive waterfront terraces.

SIHEYUAN

Traditional Beijing homes are arranged around a central courtyard. Originally homes of the well-to-do, over time many *siheyuan* were occupied by poorer families, who squeezed several households into the space formerly occupied by one. Modernization has destroyed many of these dwellings, but there is a movement to preserve those that have survived. A few have recently been converted into hotels.

TOP 10 ★ Summer Palace (Yiheyuan)

A vast landscaped park on the edge of the city, this seasonal imperial retreat from the stifling confines of the Forbidden City was the favored haunt of Empress Cixi. She had it rebuilt twice: once after its destruction by French and English troops in 1860, and again in 1902, after it was plundered during the Boxer Rebellion.

1 Hall of Happiness and Longevity

This impressive hall was the residence of the Empress Cixi. It has supposedly been left just as it was at the time of her death in 1908, complete with its Qing dynasty-era furniture.

2 Garden of Virtue and Harmony

This pretty complex of roofed corridors, small pavilions, rock gardens, and pools also includes Cixi's private three-story theater. The buildings now contain Qing-era artifacts, from vehicles to costumes and glassware.

3 Long Corridor

From the Hall of Happiness and Longevity the rather aptly named Long Corridor (left) zigzags along the shore of the lake, interrupted along its length by four pavilions. The corridor's ceilings and beams are decorated with over 14,000 scenic paintings.

Summer Palace (Yiheyuan)

4 Tower of the Fragrance of the Buddha

Toward the peak of Longevity Hill rises this octagonal tower. The stiff climb is rewarded with views over the roofs of the halls and pavilions to the lake below.

7 Temple of the Sea of Wisdom

North of the Fragrance of the Buddha Tower is a tiled temple decorated with glazed Buddhist effigies, many of which have sadly been vandalized **(left)**.

5 Longevity Hill

At around the half-way point of the Long Corridor, a series of buildings ascends the slopes of Longevity Hill **(below)**. The start of the sequence is marked at the lakeside by a fine decorative gate.

EMPRESS CIXI

Cixi is remembered as one of China's most powerful women. Having borne one emperor's son as an imperial concubine, she became the power behind the throne to two more: her son and her nephew. When she blocked state reforms and lent support to the xenophobic Boxers in their rebellion, she unwittingly paved the way for the end of the imperial era.

8 Seventeen-Arch Bridge

South Lake Island is linked to the eastern shore by a bridge **(below)** with a lion crowning each of the 544 balusters along its length, all supposedly individual. An impressive-looking bronze ox rests on the eastern shore.

6 Suzhou Street

This shopping street was built for the amusement of the Qianlong emperor, his concubines and eunuchs, who would play at being shoppers, shopkeepers, and pickpockets.

NEED TO KNOW

6 miles (10 km) NW of central Beijing ■ 6288 1144 ■ Subway: Bagou, then bus 394; Bei Gong Men ■ www.summer palace-china.com

Open Apr–Oct: 6:30am–6pm (park) daily, 8:30am–5pm (sights) daily; Nov–Mar: 7am–5pm (park) daily, 9am– 4pm (sights) daily; the last admission is two hours before closing

Adm ¥60 all inclusive, ¥30 park only; audio guides are available for ¥40 (plus ¥200 deposit)

■ There are several small snack kiosks situated in the park grounds.

■ Avoid visiting on days with poor visibility when you risk missing the superb views across the lake. These views are one of the highlights of a visit to the Summer Palace.

9 South Lake Island

Crowning this island on Kunming Lake is the Dragon King Temple (Longwang Miao), which is dedicated to the god of rivers, seas, and rain.

10 Marble Boat

The wooden structure of the boat is painted white to look like marble. Boat trips to South Lake Island depart from a neighboring jetty.

TOP 10 ⭐ 798 Art District

Since the first artists set up in Da Shan Zi's newly vacated 798 factory in 2001, the East German-built industrial compound has become a world-famous center of contemporary Chinese art. Alongside the studios and galleries, there are also chic cafés, bars, and restaurants, not to mention a growing number of designer shops and showrooms. These days the area is popular with tourists, who arrive by the coachload.

1 Maoist graffiti
When many of the abandoned factory spaces were being converted for use as galleries, the artists instructed the decorators to leave untouched the giant Maoist slogans that had been lettered on the walls by the former workers at the 798 factory.

Vibrant graffiti art in the 798 Art District

3 798 Photo Gallery
In addition to regularly changing exhibitions of work by both Chinese and foreign photographers, the gallery also has a couple of mezzanine levels where a selection of photographic prints for sale are displayed.

5 Galleria Continua
Beijing's outpost of this Italian gallery, in a former munitions factory, aims to stimulate cultural exchanges. It hosts shows by renowned international artists such as Chen Zhen, Antony Gormley, Daniel Buren, and Anish Kapoor.

2 Caochangdi
While 798 looks like a retail outlet, Caochangdi, located farther out of the city, has emerged as a truly cutting-edge art district **(above)**. It is the home of Ai Weiwei, the influential Bird's Nest architect *(see p44)*, plus Pekin Fine Arts, Egg Gallery, and Platform China.

Timezone 8 4
For post-gallery dining, Timezone 8 **(right)** serves sandwiches and burgers, plus more than 20 exotic bottled brews. The adjacent sushi bar by Hatsune genius Alan Wong offers the most creative rolls around.

798 Art District

2 km

AIRPORT EXPRESSWAY

JIU XIAN QIAO BEI LU

707 ST
706 ST

797 ROAD

718 ST
798 WEST ST
798 MIDDLE 1ST ST
798 MIDDLE 2ND ST
798 EAST ST

JIU XIAN QIAO LU

798 ROAD

QIXING RD

① ② ③ ④ ⑤ ⑥ ⑦ ⑧ ⑨ ⑩

BRAVE NEW WORLDS

1985 marked the arrival of the avant garde in Chinese art, with controversial student graduation shows igniting intense debate in artistic circles. A year later, a New York gallery introduced the new Chinese art to an international audience. Today, China's art market is the third largest in the world.

UCCA ⑦

The Ullens Center for Contemporary Art (UCCA) is the largest single venue in the 798 area **(right)**. Among the many artists showing here is Fang Lijun. UCCA has an auditorium for lectures and films, a store, and a restaurant.

⑧ Beijing Commune

This Bauhaus-style brick building has been pro-moting aspiring Chinese artists since 2004. It primarily focuses on solo performances.

⑥ AT Café

A fashionable café whose notable feature is a bare-brick dividing wall punctured by massive holes, AT serves as the unofficial canteen for the artists and gallery staff who work in the area.

⑨ Pace

This glamorous global gallery in the 798 Art District showcases the upper echelon of Chinese and Western contemporary art, and it also hosts Beijing Voice, an annual East-West art discussion between industry elites.

⑩ Magician Space

This small avant-garde gallery with a pioneering spirit has hosted a solo exhibition by the controversial Chinese artist Ai Weiwei.

NEED TO KNOW

4 Jiu Xian Qiao Lu, Chaoyang District, northeast of the Metro Park Lido complex
■ Subway: Jiangtai, then walk north for 15 min
■ Bus: 401, 402, 405, 445, 909, 955, 973, 988, 991

To Caochangdi: Bus 418 from Dong Zhi Men

Galleria Continua: 5978 9505; open 11am–6pm

Tue–Sun; www.galleria-continua.com

UCCA: 5780 0200; open 10am–7pm Tue–Sun; adm ¥60 (free on Thu); www.ucca.org.cn

Beijing Commune: 8456 2862; open 10am–6pm Tue–Sat; www.beijing commune.com

Pace: 5978 9781; www.pacegallery.com

Magician Space: 5978 9635; open 10:30am–6:30pm Tue–Sun; www.magician-space.com

■ The Ullens Center for Contemporary Art provides free maps of the entire 798 area. Most galleries are open from around 11am to 7pm, closed on Mondays.

⭐ Ming Tombs

The resting place for 13 of the 16 Ming-dynasty (1368–1644) emperors, this is China's finest example of imperial funerary architecture. The site was chosen because of its auspicious feng shui alignment: a ridge of mountains to the north cradles the tombs on three sides, protecting the dead from the evil spirits carried on the north wind. The tombs are spread over 15 square miles (40 sq km). Three (Chang Ling, Ding Ling, and Zhao Ling) have been restored and are always busy. Unrestored, the rest are open but quiet.

1 Stele Pavilion
At the tunnel-like arch of the Stele Pavilion, the largest stele in China projects from the shell of a giant bixi (dragon-tortoise) and bears the names of the emperors buried at the site.

3 Spirit Tower
Rising up from the third courtyard of the Chang Ling complex, the tower marks the entrance to the burial chamber. This takes the form of an earthen tumulus girdled by a wall.

2 Memorial Arch
Marking the entrance to the site is a five-arched marble gate (above) built in 1540. At 40 ft (12 m) high and more than 92 ft (28 m) wide, it is the largest of its kind in China, and boasts beautiful carvings.

Ming Tombs

NEED TO KNOW

30 miles (45 km) NW of Beijing ▪ 6076 1424
▪ Changping subway to Nanshao, then bus 67 to the tombs ▪ www.mingtombs.com

Open Apr–Oct 8am–5:30pm daily; Nov–Mar 8:30am–5pm daily

Adm Spirit Way ¥30, Chang Ling ¥45 (¥30 off-peak), Ding Ling ¥65 (¥45 off-peak), Zhao Ling ¥30 (¥20 off-peak)

▪ The Ming Tombs are most conveniently seen as part of a trip to the Great Wall at Badaling. Many hotels will arrange tours. The government-operated Tour Bus 2 leaves regularly for the tombs and the Great Wall from just east of Qian Men on Tian'an Men Square every day from 6:30am onward; the fare is ¥50 per person.

▪ There are snack kiosks at the site.

4 Ding Ling Burial Chamber
This is the only burial chamber to be excavated and opened to the public. Visitors descend to a central throne room and a rear annex with three red-lacquer coffins, belonging to Wanli and his two wives.

5 Chang Ling Tomb

The resting place of the Yongle emperor (the builder of the Forbidden City and Temple of Heaven) is the oldest and grandest tomb. It has been well restored, but the chamber where Yongle, his wife, and 16 concubines are buried has never been excavated.

8 Spirit Way

Part of the 4-mile (7-km) approach to the tombs, the Spirit Way is lined with 18 pairs of giant guardians (right) – stone statues of court officials, imperial warriors, animals, and mythical Chinese beasts.

6 Ding Ling Treasures

In addition to an impressive statue of the Yongle emperor, the Hall of Eminent Favor also contains artifacts from the Wanli emperor's tomb (the Ding Ling).

7 Ding Ling Tomb

This is the tomb of the longest-reigning Ming emperor, Wanli (1573–1620). His profligate rule began the downfall of the dynasty. His tomb (below) took six years to build.

9 Zhao Ling Tomb

This is the resting place of the 13th Ming emperor, Longqing (1537–72), who gained the throne at the age of 30 and died six years later. It has an attractive triple-bridge over a stream (above).

10 Hall of Eminent Favor

One of China's most impressive surviving Ming buildings, this double-eaved sacrificial hall is the centerpiece of the Chang Ling tomb complex. It stands on a triple-tiered marble terrace and 32 gigantic cedar columns support the roof.

THE MING DYNASTY

The 276-year Ming ("brilliant") dynasty rule was one of the longest and most stable periods in Chinese history. The founder of the Ming rose from humble beginnings via military successes to become emperor. He was succeeded by his grandson, who in turn was succeeded by his son, who proclaimed himself emperor Yongle ("Eternal Joy"). It was Yongle who moved the capital from Nanjing to Beijing, where he created a new city.

🔟 ⭐ Great Wall of China

The Great Wall of China snakes over deserts, hills, and plains for several thousand miles. At its closest point it is less than 40 miles (65 km) from Beijing. Created after the unification of China under Qin Shi Huangdi (221–210 BC), it ultimately proved ineffective; it

was breached in the 13th century by the Mongols and again, in the 17th century, by the Manchus. There are four main sites accessible from Beijing: Badaling, Mutianyu, Huanghua Cheng, and Simatai.

1 Badaling

The restored Ming fortification at Badaling is the closest section of the wall to Beijing. Its accessibility means it is perpetually busy. However, it is possible to escape the crowds by walking along the wall; and the views are spectacular.

Great Wall of China snaking through lush hills

2 Great Wall Museum

Housed in an imitation Qing dynasty building at Badaling, the museum **(left)** presents the history of the region from Neolithic times, as well as detailing the construction of the wall.

3 Commune by the Great Wall

Near the wall at Badaling, the Commune consists of 12 villas, each designed by a different Asian architect. The complex operates as a hotel, but non-guests can drop by for lunch, or take a tour.

NEED TO KNOW

Badaling: 44 miles (70 km) NW of Beijing; 6912 2222; Bus 877 from Desheng Men; open 7am–6pm daily; adm ¥45

Xizhazi: 60 miles (96 km) N of Beijing; Bus 936 from Dong Zhi Men bus station, to Yujiayuan station, then bus H25 to Xizhazi station

Mutianyu: 56 miles (90 km) N of Beijing; 6162 6505; Bus 916 from Dong Zhi Men bus station, change at Huairou; open 7am–6pm daily; adm ¥45

Huanghua Cheng: 37 miles (60 km) N of Beijing; 6165 1044; open 8am–5pm Mon–Fri, 7:30am–5:30pm Sat & Sun; adm ¥45

■ This area is extremely hot in summer and bitterly cold in winter. Go prepared: bring sun cream and lots of water in the warmer months, and layers in winter.

■ There are snack kiosks at each of the main four sites, but it's better to bring your own food.

4 Juyong Guan
This pass is on the way to Badaling. With unscalable mountains on either side it is easy to see why the spot was chosen for defence. Early cannons remain on the ramparts. Also worth seeing are Buddhist carvings on a stone platform, or "cloud terrace," in the middle of the pass.

VISITING THE WALL

Most hotels are able to organize a trip to the wall, usually combined with a visit to the Ming Tombs (see pp32–3). Try to find out whether there are any unwanted diversions to jade factories, cloisonné workshops, or Chinese medicine clinics. Small groups can see more remote parts of the wall, by hiring a taxi for the day from Beijing. Hiking clubs in Beijing offer day trips to lesser-known parts of the wall.

7 Xizhazi
This village in the Jiankou area affords spectacular views and accessible hikes. Xizhazi's local guesthouses offer fresh, country-style dining and a night on a traditional *kang* (heated bed).

5 Gubeikou
Once called Simatai village, this area has been redeveloped as Gubeikou, or "old town." It is a 7-mile (12-km) walk to Jinshanling, taking around five hours.

8 Shanhaiguan
The wall ends (or begins) at the sea **(above)**. East of town, the "First Pass Under Heaven" is a formidable section of wall attached to a gatehouse. A good destination if you want to do an overnight trip.

9 Mutianyu
In a dramatic hilly setting, and with a series of watchtowers along its restored length, the wall here dates from 1368. Local village buildings have now been converted into both holiday homes and restaurants.

6 Jinshanling
This is the starting point for a steep and stony hike to Gubeikou. However, the path has been blocked after 3 miles (5 km). The views as the wall winds over sharp peak after sharp peak are fantastic **(below)**.

10 Huanghua Cheng
On the same stretch of wall as Mutianyu, Huanghua Cheng is an exhilarating section of Ming fortifications that is far less developed than most other parts. The great barrier is split into two by a large reservoir. The crumbling masonry can be uneven and fairly treacherous, so you need to take care.

The Top 10 of Everything

**Performers on stage during
a Beijing Opera show**

TOP 10 Moments in History

1 500,000 BC: Peking Man Hunts and Gathers

Unearthed in the 1920s from a cave at Zhoukoudian, 30 miles (45 km) southwest of Beijing, 40-odd fossilized bones and primitive implements were identified as the remains of Peking Man (*Homo erectus Pekinensis*), who lived in the vicinity over 500,000 years ago.

2 1215: Genghis Khan Sacks Zhongdu

The future Beijing was developed as an auxiliary capital under the Liao (907–1125) and Jin (1115–1234) dynasties, at which time it was known as Zhongdu. In 1215 it was invaded and razed by a Mongol army led by the fearsome Genghis Khan.

3 Late 13th Century: Marco Polo Visits

Under the Mongol Yuan dynasty's first emperor, Kublai Khan (r. 1260–94), the city became known as Khanbalik, and was one of twin capitals – the other was Yuanshangdu, or Xanadu – of the largest empire ever known.

Kublai Khan, of the Mongol Yuan dynasty

The Venetian traveler Marco Polo was dazzled by the imperial palace:"No man on earth could design anything superior to it."

4 1403–20: Construction of the Forbidden City

The Ming emperor Yongle (r. 1403–24) destroyed the palaces of his Mongol predecessors in order to rebuild the city, which he renamed Beijing (Northern Capital). He is credited with laying the foundations for the city as it is today, and the Forbidden City and Temple of Heaven began to take shape during his reign.

5 1900: Boxer Rebellion

Western powers, frustrated by the reluctance of the Chinese to open up to foreign trade, put the imperial court under pressure, eventually going to war to protect their trade in opium. In 1900, championed by the Empress Cixi, a band of rebels known as the Boxers attacked Beijing's Foreign Legation Quarter. A joint eight-nation army had to be sent to lift the siege.

Violent clashes during the Boxer Rebellion of 1900

6 1912: The End of Empire

The last emperor, Pu Yi, was only three years old when he ascended the throne. Four years later, in February 1912, he was forced to abdicate by general Yuan Shikai's new National Assembly.

7 1949: Founding of the People's Republic of China

In January 1949, Communist forces led by Mao Zedong seized Beijing. On October 1, Mao proclaimed the People's Republic of China from the gallery of the Tian'an Men.

Mao's 1965 Cultural Revolution

8 1965: Launch of the Cultural Revolution

Having socialized industry and agriculture, Mao called on the masses to transform society itself. All distinctions between manual and intellectual work were to be abolished and the class system was to be eradicated. The revolution reached its violent peak in 1967, with the Red Guards spreading fear and havoc.

9 1976: The Death of Mao

On September 9, 1976 Mao died. His long-time opponent Deng Xiaoping became leader, implementing reforms that encouraged greater economic freedom.

10 2008: Beijing Hosts the Olympics

In 2008, Beijing hosted the Olympic Games. The city revamped its infrastructures, and some of the most striking and innovative buildings were created to house the various competitions (see pp44–5).

TOP 10 CHINESE INVENTIONS

Chinese magnetic compass

1 Porcelain
The Chinese invented porcelain 1,000 years before Europe caught on – and kept production methods secret to protect their competitive advantage.

2 Printing
In the 11th century, the Chinese carved individual characters on pieces of clay, inventing movable block type.

3 Paper money
This was developed by Chinese merchants as certificates of exchange. Lighter than coins, bills were soon adopted by the government.

4 Gunpowder
Stumbled on by Daoist alchemists seeking the elixir of life.

5 Seismometer
A ball fell from one of four dragons' mouths to indicate the direction of the earthquake.

6 Abacus
Invented during the Yuan dynasty and still in use throughout China today.

7 Magnetic compass
Developed from an instrument used for *feng shui* and geomancy, it helped the Chinese explore the world.

8 Paper
A prototype paper was made from mulberry bark, although bamboo, hemp, linen, and silk were also used to write on.

9 Crossbow
Better range, accuracy, and penetration than the standard bow.

10 Decimal system
Developed alongside the writing system, the decimal system led to mathematical advances.

🔟 Museums

3 Songtang Museum
MAP F1 ■ 3 Guozijian Jie ■ Subway: Yonghe Gong ■ Open 8:30am–6pm daily ■ Adm

A Cultural Revolution survivor, Li Songtang wanted to preserve ancient China from both political and economic destruction. Housed in a 200-year-old *hutong* courtyard home, this museum displays stone and wood carvings, plus a number of artifacts from several dynasties.

1 National Museum of China

What the British Museum is to London, the National Museum of China is to Beijing. Dedicated to Chinese history and arts, it documents the evolution of Chinese civilization through the country's most important historic and cultural artifacts. The museum hosts two permanent and numerous temporary exhibitions of art, history, and archaeology *(see p70)*.

Natural History Museum

2 Natural History Museum
There are around 5,000 specimens on display, including a fine collection of models and skeletons of dinosaurs, and other prehistoric creatures *(see p77)*.

4 Poly Art Museum
MAP G2 ■ Floor 9, New Poly Plaza, 1 Chaoyang Men Bei Dajie, Dongcheng District ■ 6500 8177 ■ Open 9:30am–4:30pm Mon–Sat ■ Adm

This museum in a central office block is cool, quiet, and packed with ancient Chinese art.

5 Imperial City Art Museum

Call by this museum near the Forbidden City to see all the bits of imperial Beijing that didn't survive. The walls and gates that once encircled the city, along with dozens of vanished temples, are revisited through a great many maps, models, and photographs *(see p70)*.

6 Beijing Police Museum
MAP M6 ■ 36 Dong Jiao Min Xiang ■ 8522 5018 ■ Subway: Qian Men ■ Open 9am–4pm Tue–Sun ■ Adm

In the 19th-century former City Bank of New York, this surprisingly fun museum has displays on themes such as the suppression of drug dealers and counter-revolutionaries. Famed police dog Feisheng is stuffed and mounted and there are live transmissions from a traffic camera. An interactive screen poses questions and correct answers win prizes.

The modern building housing the Capital Museum

7 Capital Museum

Formerly housed in the Confucius Temple, this museum now boasts a huge, modern five-story building near Fuxingmen. It documents Beijing's history through more than 200,000 relics and archival images. Among the several permanent exhibitions is the fascinating "Stories of the Capital City – Old Beijing Folk Customs" *(see p94)*.

8 National Art Museum of China

The largest art museum in the country, with an impressive 64,580 sq ft (6,000 sq m) of floor space, the National Art Museum of China hosts exhibitions by internationally renowned Chinese and foreign artists. Memorable shows have included an ethnic textile exhibition and a display by Mexican photographer Pedro Meyer *(see p70)*.

9 Ancient Architecture Museum

Close to the Temple of Heaven, south of Tian'an Men Square, this place is worth visiting for the museum building alone, which is the pavilion of a former grand temple complex *(see p77)*.

Ground floor at the Military Museum

10 Military Museum of the Chinese People's Revolution

Visitors to the museum are greeted by paintings of Mao, Marx, Lenin, and Stalin, at least two of whom were responsible for inflicting the horrific levels of death and destruction depicted within the museum. The first floor is filled with fighter planes, tanks, and missiles, while displays upstairs chronicle China's military campaigns *(see p96)*.

National Art Museum of China

TOP 10 Places of Worship

Pavilion in the Confucius Temple

1 Confucius Temple (Kong Miao)

An enormous complex of wooden halls and flagstoned courtyards, the Confucius Temple is popular with visitors and pays testament to the revival of Confucian ethics in modern China. A museum inside the temple houses artifacts of the Imperial civil service exams, and Confucian texts (see p82).

2 South Cathedral

Also known as St. Mary's Church, this was Beijing's first Catholic house of worship. It remains the largest functioning church, and has regular services in a variety of languages including Mandarin, English, and Latin. Service times are posted on the noticeboard (see p76).

3 St. Joseph's Church

MAP N3 ■ 74 Wangfujing Dajie ■ 6524 0634 ■ Subway: Dengshikou

Also known as the East Cathedral, this is a triple-domed church in the Baroque style. It was first built on the site of the residence of a Jesuit missionary in 1655 and, following earthquakes, fire, and the destruction wrought during the Boxer Rebellion, has had to be rebuilt on a number of occasions since. It is fronted by a gateway and piazza, and is beautifully lit at night.

4 Wanshou Temple

MAP A1 ■ Xisanhuan Lu, on the north side of Zizhu Qiao Bridge ■ 6845 6997 ■ Subway: Xizhi Men, then bus 300, 360, or 361 ■ Open 9am–4pm Tue–Sun ■ Adm

Up in the northwest Haidian District, the Wanshou (Longevity) Temple is worth a stop en route to the Summer Palace. The complex houses the Beijing Art Museum – a collection of historical relics including bronzes, jade, carved lacquer, and a small but exquisite collection of Buddha images.

Incense burner at Wanshou Temple

5 White Cloud Temple

Founded in AD 739, this is Beijing's largest Daoist shrine. Daoism, also known as Taoism, is a Chinese folk religion, which centers around maintaining a positive relationship with several categories of gods, ghosts, and ancestral spirits (see p95).

Facade of the Gothic North Cathedral

6 North Cathedral
MAP J2 ■ Xishiku Dajie
■ Subway: Xidan

The white-trimmed blue facade of this cathedral, a twin-towered piece of Gothic confectionery, masks a bloody past: not long after the Jesuits finished the church in 1889, it came under siege during the Boxer Rebellion. Many of the congregation sheltering inside were killed.

7 Niu Jie Mosque
There are about 200,000 Muslims in Beijing. The majority live in the Niu Jie District, which is a busy area with halal butchers, bakers, and restaurants. The mosque is the city's oldest and largest Islamic place of worship. Despite being over 1,000 years old, the mosque looks splendid, having been renovated to the tune of $2.4 million (see p76).

8 Fayuan Temple
This temple doubles as the city's Buddhist Academy. Founded in 1956, the Academy trains monks to serve in monasteries throughout China. The temple has an excellent collection of sculptures, including a giant reclining Buddha (see p74).

9 St. Michael's Church
MAP N5 ■ Dong Jiao Min Xiang
■ Subway: Chongwen Men

One of the city's less well-known churches, St. Michael's is hidden away in the old Legation Quarter (see p76). It was built in 1901, with three Gothic spires, to serve the area's various embassies. Narrowly escaping destruction during the Cultural Revolution, it was renovated by the Chinese Patriotic Catholic Church, to whom it now belongs.

10 Lama Temple
One of the most notable centers of Buddhism outside Tibet until it was shut down during the Cultural Revolution, this temple was reputedly saved from destruction by the intervention of the then president, Zhou Enlai. The precincts are home to around 70 monks (see pp20–21).

Gilded statues at the Lama Temple, an important Buddhist center

TOP10 **The Olympic Legacy**

The iconic architecture of the National Olympic Stadium (Bird's Nest)

1 Digital Beijing Building
Designed by Beijing-based Studio Pei Zhu, Digital Beijing served as the Games' Control and Data Center. It resembles a barcode from one side and an integrated circuit board from the other. It now accommodates a virtual museum and an exhibition center.

National Aquatics Center/Water Cube

2 National Aquatics Center/Water Cube
Inspired by bubbles and molecules, the dramatic-looking Water Cube is a complex of five pools. After the Olympic Games, it was transformed into a giant water park with slides and a wave pool (see p49).

3 National Indoor Stadium
Built to host gymnastics and handball during the 2008 Games, this stadium boasts a curving roof with slatted beams, inspired by Chinese folding fans. Post-Olympics, it stages entertainment events.

4 National Olympic Stadium (Bird's Nest)
Designed in collaboration with the Chinese artist Ai Weiwei, the National Olympic Stadium is an architectural icon. Its outer ribbons of structural steel resemble the woven twigs of a bird's nest as they loop and swirl over the 91,000-seat arena, hence the building's nickname.

5 Olympic Green
The vast Olympic Green surrounds the Olympic Village and extends beyond the fifth ring road. At its heart is a dragon-shaped lake, as well as waterfalls, meadows, and streams. Entry is free.

6 Olympic Green Convention Center
This building hosted the fencing events during the Games, as well as providing a home for the International Broadcasting Center. Its distinctive shape mirrors the traditional Chinese "flying roof" and acts as a giant rainwater collector. The building is now a multipurpose conference center.

7 Beijing Airport, Terminal 3
One of the world's largest and most advanced airport buildings, Lord Norman Foster's Terminal 3 welcomed international athletes to the 2008 Olympics. The design

resembles a soaring dragon in red and yellow, thus evoking traditional Chinese colors and symbols.

8 National Center for the Performing Arts
MAP K5

French architect Paul Andreu's silvery "Egg" *(see p70)* provides a striking contrast to the monolithic Socialist architecture of neighboring Tian'an Men Square. The building is surrounded by a reflective moat and accessed by an underwater tunnel. A part of the facade is transparent, so at night passers-by can see inside.

9 LeSports Center

Rebranded since the Olympics, the host venue for the basketball games features a unique exterior design that gives the impression of movement, with boards alternately rising and falling. More than mere show, the aluminum alloy boards reflect heat and reportedly result in 60–70 percent energy savings. The facility has a capacity to seat 18,000 people and is one of Beijing's largest.

10 CCTV Building
MAP H4

The most striking addition to the Beijing skyline is the headquarters of China Central Television. Designed by Dutch architects Rem Koolhaas and Ole Scheeren, it is a gravity-defying loop that pushes the limits of architecture. Its unusual design has prompted some locals to nickname the building "Glass Pants" (trousers).

CCTV Building

TOP 10 SOCIALIST MONUMENTS

Great Hall of the People

1 Agricultural Exhibition Center
MAP H2
In 1959, for the tenth anniversary of the People's Republic of China, this was one of ten buildings commissioned.

2 Great Hall of the People
MAP L5
Over 300 rooms built in 10 months.

3 National Museum of China
MAP M5
This museum is every bit as brutal and ugly as the Great Hall, which it faces across the square.

4 Beijing Railway Station
MAP F4
Prime illustration of 1959's "size is everything" approach to architecture.

5 Cultural Palace of the Nationalities
MAP C4
The one "tenth-anniversary" building of elegance. Its plan forms the Chinese character for "mountain."

6 Minzu Hotel
MAP C4
No Chinese motifs here – but it's suitably monolithic and drab.

7 Military Museum of the Chinese People's Revolution
MAP A4
Owes a striking debt to Moscow.

8 Natural History Museum
MAP E6
Neo-Classical Socialist Chinese – but fairly nice once you're inside.

9 National Art Museum of China
MAP M2
The largest art gallery in China.

10 Beijing West Railway Station
MAP A5
A 1995 take on 1959-style architecture.

🔟 Off The Beaten Path

① White Cloud Temple

Built in AD 739, Beijing's only Taoist temple houses the China Taoist Association and 30 monks with their distinctive navy-blue robes and top knots. It usually sees more pilgrims than tourists and has elaborate halls and gates, as well as three stone monkeys – finding them all is said to bring good luck (see p95).

Sundial, Ancient Observatory

Inside the Watermelon Museum

② The Watermelon Museum

Pangge Zhuang Town, Daxing District ■ 8928 1660/1181 ■ Subway: Tian Gong, then bus 28, 30 or 55 to Pangge Zhuangqiao ■ 9am–4.30pm winter; 9am–5pm summer ■ Adm

Located to the south of Beijing, the Watermelon Museum is a surrealist example of modern Socialist museums. China is the world's biggest exporter of water-melons, and self-pick farms surround this gleaming temple to the famous fruit.

③ Ancient Observatory

Located in a watchtower, this is one of the world's oldest observatories. Among the many artifacts on display are replicas of the navigational tools that enabled Ming dynasty explorers to see the world (see p89).

④ World Park

158 Dabaotai, Huaxing Township, Fengtai District ■ Subway: Dabaotai; Bus 477, 480, 692, 840, 912, 967, 969 to Shijie Gongyuan station ■ Open 9am–9pm summer; 8am–5pm winter ■ Adm, free for children under 4 ft (1.2 m)

Presenting the best of five continents in miniature form, World Park contains more than 100 replicas of world-famous cultural landmarks. These include the Egyptian pyramids and the Temple of Luxor; Rome's Colosseum and the Leaning Tower of Pisa; the Acropolis of Athens; the White House and the Statue of Liberty; and the Mogao Caves of Dunhuang.

⑤ Beijing Botanical Gardens

If the hustle and bustle of the city gets to be too much, surround yourself with Chinese roses, peach blossoms, and peonies. The massive greenhouse here displays more than 3,000 varieties of flora, ranging from tropical to desert (see p100).

Beijing Botanical Gardens in full bloom

Bronze lion at Fayuan Temple

6 Fayuan Temple

A visit to Fayuan Temple offers the opportunity to observe the fascinating daily life of a monk. Built in AD 696 by Tang dynasty emperor Tai Zong to mourn fallen soldiers, Fayuan is Beijing's largest – and likely oldest – Buddhist temple *(see p74)*.

7 Qianding Old Liquor Museum

MAP E2 ■ 69 Zhaofu Jie (near Gulou), Dongcheng District ■ 6404 0299 ■ Open 10am–6pm daily ■ Adm

This museum is all about *baijiu* (traditional grain alcohol) through the ages, and on display are more than 1,600 varieties of the stuff. The entrance is tricky to find – look for the bottles embedded in brick.

8 The Former Residence of Guo Moruo

Guo Moruo was a 20th-century writer, poet, dramatist, historian, archeologist, and paleographer, as well as an enthusiastic gardener. Much of his outdoor handiwork survives here, his former home, in addition to piles of manuscripts, books, and a bronze statue of the man himself *(see p26)*.

9 Poly Art Museum

The silent, richly carpeted rooms at the Poly Art Museum hold a wealth of stone, ceramic, and bronze statuary. Highlights include four bronze animals rescued from the 19th-century sacking of the Summer Palace, as well as artifacts ranging from the Shang to the Tang dynasties and earlier *(see p40)*.

10 Beijing Eunuch Museum (Tian Yi Mu)

80 Moshi Kou Dajie, Shijing Shan District ■ 8872 4148 ■ Subway: Pingguoyuan, then bus 959 or 746 to Shougang Xiaoqu ■ Open 9am–4pm daily ■ Adm

In the 16th century, the eunuch Tian Yi, who carried his genitals in a jug, served three emperors of the Ming dynasty. Over time, he achieved an elevated position at court, and when he died, in 1605, his funeral generated three days of silence in the Forbidden City. Tian Yi's elaborately carved tomb is now empty, having been raided during China's Cultural Revolution. However, this interesting museum houses a range of murals, monuments, marble phalluses, and a diorama of unfortunate men about to undergo the unkindest cut.

TOP10 Children's Attractions

Display at the Natural History Museum

1 Natural History Museum
As long as you steer them clear of the partially dissected human bodies, children will love this place, with its animatronic dinosaurs, prehistoric skeletons, and stuffed animals of all sizes (see p77).

2 Fundazzle
MAP G3 ■ Gongren Tiyuchang Nan Lu, south side of Workers' Stadium ■ 6593 6208 ■ Subway: Chaoyang Men ■ Open 9am–5pm Mon–Fri, 9am–7pm Sat & Sun ■ Adm

Loud and bright, this indoor kids' playground has a two-story jungle gym, a vast plastic-ball-filled pool, trampolines, swings, and a host of other activities with which to reward young children who've just had to endure a few hours of walking around the Forbidden City.

3 Beijing Aquarium
Located in the northeastern corner of the zoo, this is a very impressive attraction that will keep children happy for hours (see p97).

4 New China Children's Store
MAP N4 ■ 168 Wangfujing Dajie ■ 6528 1774 ■ Subway: Wangfujing ■ Open 9am–9:30pm daily

A four-storied children's store on Beijing's main shopping street, with everything from carry-cots and strollers to local and imported toys. There's even an in-store play area.

5 Happy Valley
Xiaowuji Bei Lu, East 4th Ring Road ■ 6738 3333 ■ Open 9:30am–10pm daily ■ Adm; children under 4 ft (1.2 m) free

This Disneyland-style park has 120 attractions over six themed regions. The park's aim is to keep both parents and children content by providing interactive education experiences. Thrill-seekers can enjoy no fewer than 40 rides, of which ten are "extreme," including a "Drop Tower" in which riders fall at 45 mph (72 km/h) in a terrifying simulated plunge to earth. There is also a shopping complex, and an IMAX cinema.

Thrilling ride at Happy Valley

Aquatic fun at the Water Cube

6 Water Cube
Olympic Park, 11 Tianchen Donglu, Chaoyang District ▪ 8437 0112 ▪ Subway: Olympic Sports Center ▪ Open 10am–9pm daily ▪ Adm; children under 4 ft (1.2 m) free

The 2008 Olympics Aquatics Center is now a water park. Water slides and giant inflatable rides will excite young fans, while the Bullet Bowl "plug hole" descent on a four-seater dinghy is a thrill for any age (see p44).

7 Blue Zoo Beijing
This small but beautifully done aquarium has an enormous coral reef tank containing an array of visually exciting marine life, including eels, rays, and sharks. Tanks are set low enough for toddlers to peer into them. There's also a "marine tunnel" and twice-daily shark-feeding sessions (see p89).

8 Chaoyang Park
Subway: Liangmaqiao

There are plenty of rides and activities here, including zip-lining, for both children and adults. This is one of the few parks in the city where visitors walk, run, do yoga, kick balls, or lay down on real grass by the lake. Go early, take a picnic, and enjoy the day.

9 Kerry Center Adventure Zone
MAP H4 ▪ Kerry Center Hotel, 1 Guanghua Lu ▪ 8565 2490 ▪ Subway: Guomao ▪ Open 10am–9pm Mon–Thu, 9am–10pm Fri–Sun ▪ Adm; ticket covers one adult and one child

Parents and children can play together at this fun center with a three-story jungle gym, a tree house, vertical slides, and colorful cars. All areas are age specific, and weary adults can always take a break and relax at the nearby café.

Science and Technology Museum

10 Science and Technology Museum
Lots of hands-on exhibits for kids to pull, push, and even walk through. There is also an IMAX-style movie theater and an indoor play area in a separate building north of the main entrance (see p101).

🔟 Entertainment

A demonstration of martial arts by Shaolin monks

1 Martial Arts
The Shaolin monks from Songshan in Henan Province have gained an international reputation for their martial arts prowess. They perform regularly at the Li Yuan Theater *(see p53)*.

2 Acrobatics
China is renowned for the quality of its gymnasts, who perform breathtaking routines that showcase their unnerving flexibility. Displays of balance often involve props such as chairs, plates, and bicycles. Several Beijing theaters put on shows – for instance, the Chaoyang Theater; your hotel can help with reservations.

Acrobats on a bicycle

3 Cinema
The easy availability of pirate DVDs means that most Beijingers watch their movies at home. Publicly screened films are subject to censorship, but foreign cultural institutes host screenings of independent and classic films. For the latest movies, head to Wanda Cineplex.

4 Puppet Theater
Shadow-puppet theater is an art form that has been performed more or less unchanged in China since the 3rd century AD. Shows employ many of the story lines and musical styles of Beijing Opera, while the puppets can be quite elaborate and colorfully dressed. The best place to catch a performance is at the China Puppet Art Theater *(Anhua Xili, off Bei Sanhuan Lu)*.

5 Rock and Pop
Beijing has a thriving music scene supported by a host of small music bars and clubs *(see p59)*. Punk and metal thrive, and for those with a more eclectic taste, local folk rockers mix ethnic instrumentation with Western genres.

6 Sports
Soccer is big in Beijing. The local boys are Beijing Guo'an, who play in the China Super League at the Workers' Stadium *(see p90)*. For

tickets, just show up at the stadium on game day. Second in popularity is basketball. The top team is Aoshen, which plays at the Beijing Guang'an Gymnasium *(Baiguang Lu; Map C6)*.

7 Traditional Music
If you can, attend a traditional Chinese orchestral performance. Sections of unfamiliar plucked string, bowed string, woodwind, and percussion instruments compete for attention in swirling arrangements. The main venues are the Forbidden City Concert Hall in Zhong Shan Park and the National Center for the Performing Arts *(see p70)*.

Performance of traditional music

8 Beijing Opera
With its incomprehensible plots, unfamiliar sounds, and performances lasting up to three hours, Beijing Opera is an acquired taste. Everyone should try it at least once *(see pp52–3)*.

9 Chinese Folk Dances
Performances showcasing China's 56 ethnic minorities, or nationalities, feature traditional costumes and dances. Some shows are truly outstanding, such as Yang Liping's famous peacock dance.

10 Theater
Beijing is home to several excellent theaters, where a few established troupes perform regularly. Canonical works such as Lao She's "Teahouse" are increasingly supplemented by big-budget Western musicals such as "Rent" and "Aladdin on Ice." See the English-language press for what's on.

TOP 10 PARKS

1 Bei Hai Park
Classic ornamental gardens with a large lake for boating *(see pp24–5)*.

2 Chaoyang Park
The largest afforested park in Beijing *(see p49)*.

3 Di Tan Park
Large green spaces and cypress trees, and the striking Altar of Earth *(see p83)*.

4 Xiang Shan Park
An hour's drive northwest of the center but worth it for thickly wooded slopes dotted with pavilions *(see p99)*.

5 Olympic Green
Subway: Forest Park
A 1,680-acre (680-hectare) green space, Beijing's largest park is home to three Olympic venues *(see p44)*.

6 Jing Shan Park
A hilly park with a pavilion providing views of the roofscape of the Forbidden City to the south *(see p71)*.

7 Long Tan Park
MAP G6 ▪ Subway: Tian Tan Dong Men
Lots of lakes, a kids' amusement park, and an enchanting water-screen show.

8 Ri Tan Park
One of Beijing's oldest parks, featuring an altar for imperial sacrifice *(see p91)*.

9 Temple of Heaven Park
This park houses several historic structures and a vast expanse of well-tended gardens, including a rose garden *(see pp16–17)*.

10 Zhong Shan Park
Just outside the walls of the Forbidden City, Zhong Shan offers a respite from the crowds *(see p71)*.

Flying kites in a Beijing park

🔟 Beijing Opera

Preparing for the role of Monkey

Not only do these characters have the most striking look of all the performers, they also usually have predominantly forceful personalities.

3 Monkey
Clever, resourceful, and brave, Monkey is one of the favorite characters in Beijing Opera. He has his origins in classic Chinese literature.

1 Colors
The colors of the performers' painted faces symbolize the individual characters' qualities. Red, for example, represents loyalty and courage. Purple stands for solemnity and a sense of justice, while green is symbolic of bravery and irascibility.

4 Dan
Dan are the female roles. *Laodan* are old ladies and *caidan* the female comedians, while *wudan* are the martial artists. The most important category, *qingyi*, usually play respectable and decent ladies in elegant costumes.

2 Jing
There are four main role types in Beijing Opera: *sheng* (male), *dan* (female), *jing* (painted face), and *chou* (clown). *Jing* have stylized patterned, colored faces, and represent warriors, heroes, statesmen, adventurers, and demons.

The comic *chou* character

5 Mei Lanfang
The foremost male interpreter of the female role (*dan*) during Beijing Opera's heyday in the 1920s and 1930s was Mei Lanfang. All female roles were once played by male actors, but this is no longer the case.

6 Chou
The *chou* are the comic characters, denoted by white patches on their noses.

Jing performers on stage

Patches of different shape and size mean roles of different character. It is the *chou* who keep the audience laughing.

7 Repertoire

The traditional repertoire includes more than 1,000 works, mostly based on popular tales. Modern productions aimed at tourists often include English-language displays of the text.

Women playing the *erhu* violin

8 Musical instruments

Despite the dramatic visual elements of Beijing Opera, the Chinese say that they go to "listen" to opera, not to see it. Typically six or seven musicians accompany the dramatics. The stringed instruments usually include the *erhu*, or Chinese two-stringed violin, while percussion includes clappers, gongs, and drums.

9 Acrobatics

Beijing Opera is a form of "total theater" with singing, speech, mime, and acrobatics that combine graceful gymnastics and martial arts movements. Training is notoriously hard. Costumes are designed to make the jumps seem more spectacular by billowing out as they spin.

10 Sheng

Sheng are divided into *laosheng*, who wear beards and represent old men, *xiaosheng* who are young men, and *wusheng*, who are the acrobats.

TOP 10 BEIJING OPERA VENUES

Show at Huguang Guild Hall

1 National Center of Performing Arts
Beijing's temple to the arts offers large-scale performances *(see p70)*.

2 Chang'an Grand Theater
MAP G4 ▪ 7 Jianguo Men Nei Dajie
▪ 6510 1308
Regular two-hour performances of mostly complete operas.

3 Mei Lanfang Grand Theater
32 Ping'Anli Xi Dajie ▪ 400 876 0505
A large steel-and-glass theater.

4 Tianqiao Performing Arts Center
MAP E6 ▪ Building 9, Tianqiao
Nandajie, Xicheng District ▪ 400
635 3355 ▪ www.tartscenter.com
A massive arts venue specializing in musical theater and traditional opera.

5 Huguang Guild Hall
MAP D5 ▪ 6304 5396 ▪ 3 Hufang Lu
Daily one-hour highlights shows.

6 Lao She Teahouse
MAP L6 ▪ 6303 6830 ▪ 3 Qian Men
Xi Dajie
Daily 90-minute variety shows.

7 Li Yuan Theater
MAP D6 ▪ 6301 6688 ▪ Qian Men
Jianguo Hotel, 175 Yong'an Lu
Daily 80-minute highlights shows.

8 Mansion of Prince Gong
MAP D2 ▪ 8328 8149 ▪ 17 Qianhai
Xi Jie
Summer performances only *(see p27)*.

9 Forbidden City Concert Hall
MAP L4 ▪ 6559 8285 ▪ West
Chang'an Avenue, Zhong Shan Park
Concert venue holding occasional opera performances.

10 Zheng Yi Temple Theater
MAP K6 ▪ 8315 1650 ▪ 220 Xiheyan
Qian Men
Weekend performances and 90-minute highlights shows.

:TOP10: **Beijing Dishes**

① Thousand-year-old Eggs

These raw duck eggs are put into mud, chalk, and ammonia and left, not for 1,000 years, but several weeks. When retrieved, the yolk and white both appear darker in color. The eggs are either sprinkled with soy sauce and sesame oil, or served in rice porridge.

② Hot Pot

Introduced to Beijing in the 13th century by the Mongols, hot pot is a much-loved staple. Hundreds of restaurants across the city sell this dish. Everybody sits around a large bubbling pot of broth dropping in their own shavings of meat, noodles, and vegetables to cook.

Whole roasted Beijing duck

Mongolian fire hot pot

③ Zha Jiang Mian

The name means "clanging dish noodles" – like hot pot, ingredients are added at the table to a central tureen of noodles, and the bowls are loudly clanged together as each dish goes in, hence the name.

④ Beijing Duck

This is arguably one of the best-known dishes in north Chinese cuisine. The duck, a local Beijing variety, is dried and brushed with a sweet marinade before being roasted over fragrant wood chips. It is carved by the chef and then eaten wrapped in pancakes with slivered scallions (spring onions) and cucumber.

⑤ La Mian

Watching a cook make *la mian* (hand-pulled noodles) is almost as enjoyable as eating them. First the dough is stretched and then swung like a skipping rope, so that it becomes plaited. The process is repeated several times, until the strands of dough are as thin as string.

⑥ Sweet and Sour Carp

Beijing cooking is heavily influenced by the cuisine of Shandong Province, generally regarded as the oldest and best in China. Sweet and sour carp is a quintessential Shandong dish traditionally made with fish from the Yellow River.

Zha jiang mian

7 Stir-fried Kidney Flowers
These are pork kidneys cut in a criss-cross fashion and stir-fried, during which they open out like "flowers." The kidneys are typically prepared with bamboo shoots, water chestnuts, and edible black fungus.

8 Drunken Empress Chicken
This dish is supposedly named for Yang Guifei, an imperial concubine who was overly fond of her alcohol. The dish is prepared using Chinese wine and is served cold.

Steamer stacked with various dumplings

9 Jiaozi
Traditional Beijing dumplings are filled with pork, *bai cai* (Chinese leaf), and ginger but, in fact, fillings are endless. You can find *jiaozi* at snack shops all over the city. They are also sold on the street, either steamed or fried on a giant hot plate over a brazier.

10 Lamb and Scallions
Scallions (spring onions) are a common Beijing ingredient and in this dish they are rapidly stir-fried along with sliced lamb, garlic, and a sweet-bean paste.

TOP 10 BEIJING STREET FOODS

1 Lu da gun'r
Literally "donkeys rolling in dirt": sweet red-bean paste in a rice dough dusted with peanut powder.

2 Jian bing
A Chinese crêpe often sold off the back of tricycles. It is a typical Beijing breakfast dish.

3 Shao bing
Hot bread roll sometimes filled with a fried egg and often sprinkled with aniseed for flavoring.

4 Tang chao lizi
Chestnuts, roasted in sugar and hot sand and served in a paper bag. A seasonal snack appearing in autumn.

5 Tang hu lu
A kebab of candied hawthorn berries.

6 Chuan'r
In any area with lots of bars and clubs you'll find street vendors selling *chuan'r* (kebabs). They cost just a few *yuan* per skewer.

7 Baozi
These delicious steamed dumplings are cooked in bamboo baskets. Typical fillings include pork, chicken, beef, or vegetables and tofu.

8 Rou bing
Cooked bread filled with finely chopped and spiced pork. A variant is *rou jiamo*, which is a bun packed with finely diced lamb.

9 You tiao
Deep-fried dough sticks, often dipped in warm congee (a rice porridge).

10 Hong shu
A winter specialty, these are baked sweet potatoes, often heated in ovens made from oil drums.

Skewered berries in a *tang hu lu*

🔟 Restaurants

Relaxed ambience at Mosto, an international bistro in Sanlitun

① Mosto
MAP H2 ▪ Nali Patio, 81
Sanlitun Bei Lu ▪ 5208 6030 ▪ ¥¥¥
Serving contemporary classics, Mosto
has plenty of fans thanks to its great
wine list and immaculate service.

② Georg
45 Dongbuyaqiao Hutong, nr
Dianmen Dajie ▪ 8408 5300 ▪ ¥¥¥
Fine dining from the eponymous
Danish silverware brand, complete
with minimalist design and a nearby
babbling brook. Sample the wine
pairing and tasting menus.

Elegant dining at Georg

③ Din Tai Fung
24 Xinyuan Xili Middle Street
▪ 6462 4502 ▪ ¥¥
This place specializes in southern
Chinese dishes, particularly the light,
fresh flavors of Zhejiang and Jiangsu

provinces. Try the house special
xialong bao, juicy buns filled with
pork or seafood prepared in a
bamboo steamer, or the steamed
dumplings with vegetables.

④ Temple Restaurant
MAP M2 ▪ 23 Shatan Beijie
▪ 8400 2232 ▪ Subway: Dong Si
Shi Tiao ▪ ¥¥¥
Located in a beautifully restored
600-year-old temple complex,
this upmarket restaurant offers
high-quality European cuisine.
Advance reservations are essential.

⑤ The Orchid
MAP E2 ▪ 65 Baochao Hutong,
Dongcheng District ▪ 8404 4818
▪ Open daily ▪ ¥¥¥
The Orchid gained fame as a stylish
hotel at the end of a winding *hutong*,
but its Middle Eastern-inspired menu
also has patrons raving. Come for
dinner, stay for a drink, and soak
up the atmosphere *(see p115)*.

⑥ Lost Heaven
Located in the former US
embassy, this restaurant has plenty
of authentic touches from the
southwestern province of Yunnan.
This is the most foreign-friendly
of the Chinese cuisines, and it is
famous for its local cheese *(see p79)*.

(7) Dali Courtyard
Beautifully lit by candles at night, this atmospheric courtyard venue wins top marks for ambience, as well as for its excellent set menus made up of classic dishes from Yunnan province. It's a good idea to reserve a table *(see p85)*.

(8) Country Kitchen
MAP H3 ■ Rosewood Beijing, Jingguang Centre, 1 Chaoyangmen Dajie ■ 6597 8888 ■ ¥¥¥
Featuring northern dishes such as beef brisket, duck and black mushroom sauce, as well as Sichuan ones, like fiery chicken and prawns.

(9) Mercante
4 Fangzhuanchang Hutong, Dongcheng District ■ 8402 5098 ■ ¥¥¥
Mercante brings a Mediterranean vibe to Beijing's *hutongs*, with handmade pasta, home-made ricotta cheese, and organic beef. Good cooking takes time, but sip on some quality wines and enjoy the evening.

(10) Cai Yi Xuan
MAP H1 ■ Four Seasons Beijing, 48 Liang Ma Qiao Lu ■ 5695 8520 ■ ¥¥¥
Enjoy some of Beijing's best dim sum, along with high-end Cantonese fare such as sea cucumber, abalone, and seasonal hairy crab.

Refined table setting at Cai Yi Xuan

TOP 10 CHEAP EATS

Steamed dumplings

1 Mr Shi's Dumplings
MAP E1 ■ 4 Cheniandian Hutong, Anding Men Dajie
MSG-free dumplings and local dishes served by English-speaking staff.

2 Ling Er Jiu Noodles
Building 1, 6 Fangyuan Xilu
Noodles and braised pork sandwiches.

3 Pingwa Sanbao
10A Xiangjunzhuang Lu
Pingwa offers hand-pulled noodles and *chuan'r* (kebabs).

4 Green Bites Dumpling Bar
E166, Tower E, World City, 8–9 Jinhui Lu
Socially responsible dumplings, with eco-friendly carry-out boxes.

5 Mama de Weidao
6–110 Zhongguo Hong Jie Building, 2 Gongti Dong Lu
Home-style northern cuisine.

6 Southern Fish
166 Yang Mei Zhu Xie Jie
The impossibly spicy Hunan food here attracts plenty of locals; reserve ahead.

7 Nice Rice
23 Dongsiertiao, Dongcheng
Hunan cuisine in modern surrounds; try stir-fried tofu and fiery beef dishes.

8 Zhang Mama
76 Jiaodoukou Nan Dajie
This is the place for hot Sichuan snacks; even the scrambled eggs are packed with chili.

9 Yun-er Small Town
84 Beiluoguxiang
Yunnan fare on a rooftop terrace; try the potatoes cooked with tea leaves.

10 Tiger Mama
Building 38, Sanlitun Xijie
Macanese shop offering wet or dry noodles, fish balls, and beef offal.

For a key to restaurant price ranges see p73

⏹️10 Bars and Pubs

Ingredients for cocktails at Manhattan-style bar Janes and Hooch

① Janes and Hooch
MAP H2 ▪ Courtyard 4, Gongti Bei Lu ▪ 6503 2757 ▪ Subway: Tuanjiehu

Cocktails, bourbons, and ales are served at this split-level speakeasy bar and lounge to the accompaniment of smooth jazz and blues music.

② Botany Bar
MAP H2 ▪ 1209 Unit 2, Yonglee Plaza, Gongti Bei Lu ▪ 6463 6091

Swanky yet homey apartment bar with work-of-art cocktails such as Amortentia, infused with rosemary sprigs and toasted sesame seeds.

③ La Social
MAP H2 ▪ 3rd Floor, Nali Patio, 81 Sanlitun Lu ▪ 5208 6030

This is a Columbian bar with serious food options, including *arepas* (corn

flatbreads with varied fillings), and excellent cocktails. The eclectic decor includes a picture of Jesus framed by yellow bulbs, velvet lampshades, and neon busts of Mao.

Pina colada cocktail

④ Mai
A smartly designed cocktail bar, Mai has outdoor seating in a narrow courtyard, plus a giant silver sofa and bar chairs inside. It draws a cool *hutong* crowd, especially at weekends *(see p84).*

⑤ Migas
MAP H2 ▪ 6/F Nali Patio, 81 Sanlitun Bei Lu ▪ 5208 6061 ▪ Subway: Tuanjiehu

This chic Spanish restaurant and rooftop terrace bar is always packed with a hip cocktail-drinking crowd that comes here for the DJs and great alfresco views. Try the chargrilled octopus.

⑥ Hidden House
MAP H2 ▪ 39 Xin Dong Lu, Chaoyang District ▪ 8418 5718

The cozy alcoves at this utterly charming speakeasy are perfect for quiet conversation and the cocktails are new takes on old favorites.

Fried *arepas* at La Social

7 The Tree
MAP H2 ■ 43 Sanlitun Bei Jie ■ 6415 1954 ■ Subway: Dong Si Shi Tiao

A favorite among expats, this is a convivial pub with a fantastic array of beers (40 Belgian brews alone) and excellent wood-fired pizzas.

Wood-fired pizza at The Tree

8 Amilal
48 Shoubi Hutong, Dongcheng District ■ 8404 1416

This Mongolian-owned whiskey bar in a tiny *hutong* has it all – a mishmash of comfortable furniture, random cultural artifacts, tiny tables, hushed conversation, and a number of roaming cats.

9 Centro
MAP H4 ■ Kerry Center Hotel, 1 Guanghua Lu ■ 6561 8833 ext. 6296 ■ Subway: Guomao

Set in the lobby of one of the city's swankiest hotels, Centro boasts live jazz and the last word in cocktails.

Tables on the deck terrace at Mesh

10 Mesh
MAP H2 ■ B1, The Opposite House, 11 Sanlitun Bei Lu ■ 6410 5220 ■ Subway: Tuanjiehu

Ultra-trendy lounge bar Mesh features a cool outdoor deck terrace and bamboo garden. It's a popular spot for after-work cocktails and evening drinks on weekends.

TOP 10 MUSIC BARS

1 Dusk Dawn Club
14 Shanlao Hutong, Dongcheng District ■ 6407 8969
Courtyard venue with trees growing through tables and regular live shows.

2 School Live Bar
53 Wudaoying Hutong, Dongcheng District ■ 6402 8881
This *hutong* venue is one of the city's best music spots.

3 Jianghu Bar
MAP E2 ■ 7 Dongmianhua Hutong, Jiaodaokou Nan Dajie ■ 6401 5269
Cozy courtyard bar hosting jam sessions.

4 Blue Note
MAP M6 ■ 23 Qian Men Dong Dajie ■ 6527 0288
The jazz club's first branch in China.

5 Dada
MAP E2 ■ 183 1108 0818 ■ 206 Gulou Dong Dajie
Super-hip DJ lounge and mini club import from Shanghai.

6 Hot Cat Club
MAP F1 ■ 6400 7868 ■ 46 Fangjia Hutong
This compact pub is the mainstay of Beijing's live Indie music scene.

7 Modernista
A 1920s-themed jazz and piano bar that also serves Spanish tapas *(see p84)*.

8 Temple Bar
MAP E2 ■ 206 Gulou Dong Dajie ■ 131 6107 0713
This institution has live shows, a wide drink selection and late-night pub food.

9 East Shore Live Jazz Cafe
A classic pure jazz venue with terrific views over Hou Hai *(see p84)*.

10 Yugong Yishan
3-2 Zhangzizhong Lu ■ 6404 2711
The city's most satisfying music venue, with an eclectic booking policy.

Jianghu Bar's rustic interior

Markets and Shops

Pearls at Hong Qiao Market

1 Hong Qiao Market

Hong Qiao is best known for pearls (hence its alternative name, the "Pearl Market"), with a huge range available, freshwater and seawater, up on the third floor. The floors below are a tight compress of clothing, shoes, electronics, and more, while in the basement is a pungent, but fascinating, market for fish, frogs, and snakes *(see p78)*.

2 Oriental Plaza

A large mall that stretches a whole city block and features several levels of top-end retailers including Paul Smith, Swarovski, Sisley, Max Mara, and Apple. There is also a Watsons drugstore, a big CD and DVD store, and an excellent food court *(see p72)*.

3 Zhongguancun, Electronics Avenue

Subway: Wudaokou, then taxi
Zhongguancun is the capital's technology hub, and Electronics Avenue is home to some of the biggest electronics markets in Beijing. Stores sell everything from laptops and iPhones to DSLR cameras. Staff rarely speak English, so bring a printout of the model you want.

4 Plastered T-Shirts

MAP E2 ■ 61 Nan Luogu Xiang, Dongcheng District ■ 6406 4872 ■ Open 9:30am–11pm daily
A great place for gifts, Plastered offers quirky Beijing style in the form of T-shirts and tote bags. Founder Dominic Johnson Hill works with Chinese designers, and everything is manufactured in the capital. There is another shop in the 798 Art District.

5 Three Stone Kite Shop

MAP K1 ■ 25A Di'an Men Xi Dajie, Xicheng District ■ 8404 4505 ■ Open daily
Proprietor and craftsman Liu Bin comes from a long line of kite makers, some of whom once served the royal family. His kites are true works of art. Sturdy enough for Beijing breezes, they also make exquisite – and lightweight – gifts. The shop runs kite-making classes, too.

Taikoo Li Sanlitun shopping center

6 Taikoo Li Sanlitun

This hip shopping, dining, and entertainment center in Sanlitun features numerous colored glass buildings housing over 200 stores, including global brand flagships such as the Apple Store and Nike, plus some of downtown Beijing's best bars and cafés *(see p92)*.

7 Panjiayuan Antique Market

As much a tourist attraction as a shopping experience, Panjiayuan is home to around 3,000 dealers peddling everything from broken bicycles to family heirlooms. Come here for Mao memorabilia, a Qing-dynasty vase, or Tintin comics in Chinese. Panjiayuan Market is at its busiest and best on weekends. Serious collectors swoop at dawn, but it's fun any time of the day *(see p78)*.

8 Cathay Bookshop (Zhongguo Shudian)
Liulichang Xi Jie ▪ 6317 3805 ▪ Open 9am–5:30pm daily

A bookstore with a vast selection of modern Chinese art books, as well as classic second-hand, vintage, and antique collections.

9 Beijing Postcards
97 Yangmeizhuxiejie ▪ 156 1145 3992 ▪ www.bjpostcards.com

This fascinating shop sells historic Beijing postcards, maps, calendars, and prints from the 1870s–1940s, all purchased at auction or from descendants of missionaries. See the website for information on their lectures and historical walking tours.

Colorful fabrics at the Silk Market

10 Silk Market

Properly known as Xiushui, this market is reportedly one the city's most popular tourist attractions – after the Forbidden City and the Great Wall. The bargains are not what they used to be, but some 100,000 shoppers a day still visit to snap up famous brand goods *(see p92)*.

Panjiayuan Antique Market

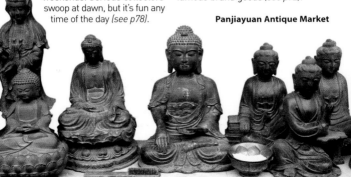

🔟 Beijing for Free

1 Museums
Many of Beijing's big national museums – including the Natural History Museum *(see p77)*, the National Museum of China *(see p70)*, and the National Art Museum of China *(see p70)* – offer free entry, although you may be asked to pay a small fee for an optional guide. The Capital Museum *(see p94)* is free but requires you to make an online reservation before you visit.

2 Former Residence of Lao She
MAP M3 ▪ 19 Fengfu Lane, Dengshikou Xije, Dongcheng District ▪ 6514 2612 ▪ Subway: Dengshikou ▪ Open 8am–6pm daily
This well-preserved courtyard home with a memorial honors Beijing personality and Chinese luminary Lao She, author of such literary classics as *Teahouse* and *Rickshaw Boy*.

3 Beijing University Campus
5 Yiheyuan Road, Haidian District ▪ 0506 5075 ▪ Subway: Peking University (East Gate)
Known locally as PKU (Peking University), Beijing University is a sprawling campus, complete with a willow-lined lake. It also features Haidian's best theater venue.

4 Southern Moat and Central Axis
MAP E6 (Southern Moat) ▪ Access to Southern Moat via Yongdingmen Gate ▪ Access to Central Axis via Yonghe Gong Park
Beijing's once-extensive moat network has been diminished by centuries of war, structural changes, and a drying climate. Still, walking the footpath along the palace's Southern Moat is a peaceful trip back to the old city.

5 Panjiayuan Antique Market
Once called the "dirt market," when farmers used to literally unearth treasures and bring them to sell, today Panjiayuan is where you'll find all sorts of antiques, from carved furniture to propaganda art and Qing-dynasty pottery *(see p78)*.

Statuary at Panjiayuan Antique Market

6 Meridian Space
MAP N2 ▪ 77 Meishuguan Houjie, Dongcheng District ▪ 8105 6788 ▪ Open 10am–7pm daily ▪ Call ahead to visit Ma Ke's showroom
Located in a retro-chic brick factory, Meridian Space is an events venue housing a folk-art exhibition and designer Ma Ke's showroom. Her Wu Yong (meaning "useless") label uses traditional dyeing, weaving, and intricate embroidery techniques.

Leafy grounds at Beijing University Campus

Charming Beijing *hutong*

7 Hutongs

Hutongs, or traditional lanes, are where you'll find Beijing's old-world charm. Try Nanluoguxiang and Beiluoguxiang *hutongs*, near Gulou; Fangjia and Wudaoying *hutongs*, across from the Lama Temple; and Dashilan *hutong* in the Qian Men area.

8 Street Dancing

The so-called "dancing grannies" are senior citizens who meet in public squares for socializing and light exercise, whether it be fans and drumming, ballroom dancing, or low-key aerobics. This is one of Beijing's more charming features.

9 Yishu 8

MAP M2 ■ **20 Dong Huangchengen Bei Jie, Dongcheng District** ■ **6581 9058** ■ **Subway: Dongsi, Nanluoguxiang** ■ **Open 11am–6:30pm Mon–Sat** ■ **www. yishu-8.com**

Housed in the old Sino-French University, Yishu 8 hosts regular exhibitions featuring cross-cultural collaborations of Chinese and French artists. Each room has its own style, and the leafy courtyard offers welcome respite from the city.

10 Maliandao (Tea Street)

There's little charm about Maliandao, which is basically a tea mall for wholesalers. However, here you can see, smell, and learn everything you ever wanted to know about tea. There's an impressive range of flower types, and you can enjoy unlimited free samples on all three floors *(see p78)*.

TOP TEN BUDGET TIPS

1 Tickets
Research museums and other sights online to decide which to visit. For some sights, you can buy an all-access pass or a single-zone pass.

2 Public Transport
Forget taxis; the Beijing subway costs only ¥4. Subway cards offer a 60 percent discount on buses.

3 Airport Transit
Upon disembarking, catch the airport express (¥25), then transfer to a bus or subway at Dong Zhi Men.

4 Street Food
Eating delicious *chuan'r* (roasted kebabs) or *malatang* (boiled kebabs) paired with a ¥2 local beer will be a highlight of your stay in Beijing.

5 Museums
On Wednesdays, 13 museums offer free admission to the first 200 visitors.

6 Public Spectacle
Dancing or doing tai chi with the locals costs nothing, and the experience will create a priceless memory.

7 Self-Restraint
Markets are exercises in bargaining, but the best deals come before closing time, so be sure to pace yourself.

8 Dorm Life
Opt for a hostel over a hotel; beds are cheap, and the hostel locations are among the best in the city.

9 Two-Wheelers
Travel like a local and rent a bicycle, or register for public bicycles on the street. Cycle on a quiet side street first.

10 Connections
Every café has free Wi-Fi, and WeChat offers free international texts, voice messages, and phone calls.

Rack of public bicycles

🔟 **Festivals and Events**

Fireworks and traditional dances heralding Chinese New Year

① **Chinese New Year**
Three days from the 1st day of the 1st moon, usually late Jan or early Feb
Also known as Spring Festival, Beijing's favorite holiday sees fireworks let off night and day across the city, plus temple fairs with stilt-walkers, acrobats, and fortune-tellers. Families make *jiaozi* (dumplings) together and exchange gifts, then the adults watch the annual Spring Festival Gala on television.

② **Lantern Festival**
The 15th day of the lunar calendar (end of Feb)
This festival marks the end of the 15-day Spring Festival celebrations. Lanterns bearing auspicious characters or in the shape of animals are hung everywhere. It is also a time for eating the sticky rice balls known as *yuanxiao*.

Lantern Festival

③ **Tomb-Sweeping Festival (Qing Ming)**
Apr 5, but Apr 4 in leap years
On this public holiday, Chinese families visit their ancestors' graves to tidy them up, make offerings of snacks and alcohol, and burn incense and paper money.

④ **International Labor Day**
May 1
Labor Day is celebrated with a three-day holiday, which marks the start of the domestic travel season. Shops, offices, and other businesses close for the entire holiday, and often for a whole week. Don't plan on doing any out-of-town travel during this time.

⑤ **Dragon Boat Festival (Duanwu Jie)**
The 5th day of the 5th lunar month (early Jun)
Drums thunder as dragon-headed craft compete for top honors. The festival remembers the honest official, Qu Yuan, who drowned himself 2,500 years ago after banishment from the court of the Duke of Chu. Citizens threw rice cakes into the water to distract the fish from nibbling on his body, hence the wholesale consumption of these delicacies on this date.

Dragon Boat Festival competition

6 Chinese Valentine's Day
The 7th day of the 7th lunar month (usually Aug)

This festival celebrates the forbidden love between a mortal and a goddess. Couples exchange gifts, and single women take fruit or flowers to a temple and pray for love.

7 Mid-Autumn Festival
The 15th day of the 8th lunar month (usually Sep)

Also known as the Harvest or Moon Festival, this is traditionally a time for family reunions and for giving boxes of sweet and savory mooncakes (yuebing).

8 Cricket-Fighting
Mid-Sep to the end of Oct

The Chinese version of cricket involves ruthless antennae-on-antennae action as cricket-fanciers goad their insects into battle in the plastic bowls that serve as gladiatorial arenas. Once the favorite sport of emperors, it now takes place in backstreets all over town.

National Day on Tian'an Men Square

9 National Day
Oct 1

On the anniversary of the foundation of the People's Republic, crowds turn out to watch military parades in Tian'an Men Square, which is colored red by a sea of waving flags.

10 Christmas Day
Dec 25

Not a traditional Chinese holiday but the festivities have been adopted via Hong Kong, which means that the focus is on squarely consumerism.

TOP 10 CULTURAL EVENTS

1 Temple Fairs
Jan/Feb
Colorful street fairs outside the city's large temples during Chinese New Year.

2 Longqing Gorge Ice Festival
MAP G5 ▪ Longqing Gorge ▪ Jan & Feb
Showcases giant ice and snow sculptures illuminated by pretty colored lights in a rural setting 25 miles (40 km) northwest of Beijing (see p105).

3 Surge
Spring and autumn
Emerging artists' exhibitions take place at the Red Gate Gallery (see p90).

4 Beijing International Film Festival
Various venues ▪ Apr
This is China's largest film festival.

5 Meet in Beijing Festival
Apr–Jun
A festival of theater, dance, and music by groups from several continents.

6 Art Beijing
National Agricultural Exhibition Center ▪ May
Contemporary art fair with exhibitors from around the globe.

7 Croisements Festival
May–Jun
Festival blending French and Chinese culture, often on the same stage.

8 NLGX Performing Arts Festival
Jun–Aug
International players perform in venues in Nan Luogu Xiang (see p81).

9 Beijing Dance Festival
Jul
Established modern dance companies perform alongside emerging talent.

10 Beijing Music Festival (BMF)
Oct
Featuring the biggest names in music.

Opera, Meet in Beijing Festival

Beijing
Area by Area

High-rises reflected on the water in
Beijing's Central Business District

TOP 10 Tian'an Men Square and the Forbidden City Area

The geographical, spiritual, and historical heart of Beijing, Tian'an Men Square and the Forbidden City together represent a yin and yang arrangement; one is a vast, empty public space, the other is an even larger walled enclosure. One represents modern China, while the other is a silent repository of ancient imperial glories. It is worth setting aside a whole day for each. Afterward, wander around the corner for a look at the National Center for the Performing Arts and a glimpse of the China of the future.

Vase at the National Museum of China

1 Tian'an Men Square

Although now synonymous with Beijing, until relatively recently there was no Tian'an Men Square. For centuries this was just a main thoroughfare leading to the Gate of Heavenly Peace (Tian'an Men). Cleared in the first half of the 20th century, the area quadrupled in size in 1959, supposedly allowing for up to one million people to gather. Many of the buildings on the square were erected at this time (see pp18–19).

The vast Great Hall of the People

2 Great Hall of the People

MAP L5 ■ West side of Tian'an Men Square ■ 6605 6847 ■ Subway: Tian'an Men West ■ Opening hours vary ■ Adm

This is the parliament building, home of China's legislative body, the National People's Congress. Tours visit the banquet room and the 10,000-seat auditorium, with its ceiling inset with a massive red star. The building is closed to the public when the Congress is in session.

- **1** Top 10 Sights
  see pp68–71
- **1** Restaurants
  see p73
- **1** Shops and Venues
  see p72

3 Forbidden City

The Forbidden City is Beijing's top "must-see" sight. A seemingly endless collection of pavilions, gates, courts, and gardens, this majestic complex encompasses five centuries of colorful – and occasionally lurid – imperial history. Until the mid-1900s, only members of the imperial court were allowed inside – hence the name. Trying to see everything in one go will bring on a severe case of Ming fatigue, and it is highly recommended that you tackle this wonderful palace over at least two separate visits (see pp12–15).

Bronze lion at the Forbidden City

TIAN'AN MEN SQUARE AND THE FORBIDDEN CITY AREA

4 Imperial City Art Museum

MAP M5 ■ 9 Changpu Heyan ■ 8511 5104 ■ Subway: Tian'an Men East ■ Open 10am–5:30pm Tue–Sun ■ Adm ■ Audio tour available for a fee

Much of Beijing's Imperial City was destroyed under the Communists. A model in this museum shows just how much has been lost, including the wall that once encircled the city and many temples. There are also collections of armor and ceramics.

Fountain at Wangfujing Dajie

5 Wangfujing Dajie

MAP N4 ■ Subway: Wangfujing

One of downtown Beijing's most famous shopping precincts, Wangfujing Dajie is filled with department stores, restaurants, and malls (see p72), as well as several bookshops and stores selling silk, tea, and shoes. To the north is St. Joseph's, one of the city's most important churches (see p42).

6 National Art Museum of China

MAP M2 ■ 1 Wusi Dajie ■ 8403 3500 ■ Subway: Dong Si Shi Tiao ■ Open 9am–5pm daily ■ Audio guides available for a fee ■ www.namoc.org

China's largest art gallery was one of ten key buildings erected in 1959 to celebrate the tenth anniversary

THE CULT OF MAO

Mao Zedong was an ideologue whose impatience at the pace of reform often brought disaster, yet skillful maneuvering by the Party meant that he remained a heroic figure. Mao's status diminished in the years after his death as his influence was overshadowed by the political and economic reforms carried out by Deng Xiaoping and other leaders.

of the founding of the People's Republic. Its 14 halls, spread over three floors, host a constant rotation of temporary exhibitions of Chinese and international art.

7 National Museum of China

MAP M5 ■ East side of Tian'an Men Square ■ 6511 6400 ■ Subway: Tian'an Men East ■ Open 9am–5pm Tue–Sun ■ www.chnmuseum.cn

Combining the original Museum of Chinese History and the Museum of the Revolution, this huge space offers an unsurpassed collection of Chinese artworks and other historical, archaeological, and cultural objects. There are also models, documents, and photographs connected with the history of the Chinese Communist Party – for political enthusiasts only. The museum also hosts temporary exhibitions.

8 National Center for the Performing Arts

MAP K5 ■ 2 West Chang An Jie ■ 6655 0000 ■ Subway: Tian'an Men West ■ www.chncpa.org

This modern opera house, a major landmark on Beijing's skyline, hosts a year-round program of opera, theater, and concerts. Designed by French architect Paul Andreu, it is

National Center for the Performing Arts

built of glass and titanium and takes the form of a giant parabolic dome – earning it the nickname "The Egg." Entrance to the building is through an underwater tunnel.

⑨ Jing Shan Park

MAP L2 ■ 1 Wenjin Jie ■ 6404 4071 ■ Bus: 5, 111, 124, 810 ■ Open 6am–9pm daily ■ Adm

Jing Shan (Coal Hill) lies north of the Forbidden City. The hill, created from the earth that was excavated while building the moat around the palace complex, was meant to protect the emperor and his court from malign northern influences, which brought death and destruction according to *feng shui*. The park is dotted with pavilions and halls, but the highlight is the view over the Forbidden City from the hilltop Wancheng Pavilion.

View from the hill of Jing Shan Park

⑩ Zhong Shan Park

MAP L4 ■ 6605 5431 ■ Subway: Tian'an Men West ■ Open 6am–9pm daily ■ Adm ■ www.zhongshan-park.cn

Northwest of the Tian'an Men, Zong Shan (also known as Sun Yat Sen Park) offers respite from the crowds thronging the nearby sights. The park was once part of the grounds of a temple, and the square Altar of Earth and Harvests remains. In the eastern section is the Forbidden City Concert Hall, Beijing's premier venue for classical music.

A DAY AROUND TIAN'AN MEN SQUARE AND WANGFUJING DAJIE

▶ MORNING

Arrive early to beat the crowds at **Mao's Mausoleum** *(see p19)* and shuffle through for the permitted few minutes in the presence of the Great Helmsman. The Forbidden City can be saved for another day, but climb the **Tian'an Men** *(see p18)* for the views from the gallery. From the gate, walk east along the Imperial City wall, soon arriving at an entrance over-looked by most visitors: this leads to the **Imperial Ancestral Temple**, an ancient place of worship. Take a walk through **Zhong Shan Park** and stop by the box office to check about concert tickets before heading east to **Wangfujing Dajie** and the **Oriental Plaza** mall *(see p60)*. Browse Beijing's first ritzy shopping district, then hit **Haidilao Hot Pot** *(see p73)* for lunch.

AFTERNOON

Wander up **Wangfujing Dajie**, making sure to look in the chopstick and tea shops. At No. 74 is the attractive **St. Joseph's Church**, which is well worth a look. Immediately before the church is a crossroads: head away from the church along Deng Shi Kou Jie looking for signs for Fengfu Hutong on your right. Here is the **Former Residence of Writer Lao She** *(see p62)*, offering a glimpse into a way of life fast disappearing in Beijing. Keep heading north to **Susu** *(see p73)*, for a Vietnamese dinner in a converted courtyard.

See map on pp68–9 ⬅

Shops and Venues

1 Oriental Plaza
MAP N5 ▪ 1 Dong Chang'an Jie
Several floors of high-end, big-name international retailers, from Apple and Sony to designers such as Armani and Paul Smith. Don't expect to find any bargains.

2 Foreign Languages Bookstore
MAP N4 ▪ 235 Wangfujing Dajie
Most of the first floor here is devoted to English-language fiction and non-fiction works and the staff are reliably surly.

3 Ten Fu's Tea
MAP N4 ▪ 88 Wangfujing Dajie ▪ www.tenfu.com
Tea from all over China is sold loose or in beautiful presentation boxes at this lovely shop. Staff will even brew small cups for sampling.

4 APM
MAP N4
▪ 138 Wangfujing Dajie
This shopping mall full of mid-range clothes shops also has a multiscreen cinema as well as plenty of restaurants on the top floor.

5 Beijing Arts & Crafts Central Store
MAP N4 ▪ 200 Wangfujing Dajie
A vast, multistory emporium of all kinds of handicrafts, from cloisonné vases and jade to wood carvings, lacquer ware, and silks.

6 Mao's Mausoleum
MAP L5 ▪ Tian'an Men Square ▪ Subway: Qian Men ▪ Open 8:30–11:30am Mon–Sat, 2–4pm Mon, Wed & Fri
The mausoleum gift shop is the best source of Mao badges, posters, and shoulder bags.

7 Forbidden City Concert Hall
MAP L4 ▪ West Chang'an Avenue, Zhong Shan Park ▪ 6559 8285
This venue draws the best musicians in town. In summer, the Gateway to Music Festival sees big names and traditional music concerts *(see p53)*.

8 Capital Theater
MAP N4 ▪ 22 Wangfujing Dajie ▪ 6553 3969
The city's smartest theater plays classic Chinese dramas, plus the occasional foreign Shakespeare show, to captivated audiences.

9 Hao Yuan Market
MAP N4 ▪ Off Wangfujing Dajie
A small street market just off Wangfujing, Hao Yuan is crammed with stalls selling knick-knacks, local handicrafts, and curios.

10 Intime Lotte
MAP N4 ▪ 88 Wangfujing Dajie
This high-end mall is jointly owned by the Korean department giant Lotte and the Chinese Intime group. It also hosts cultural events and exhibitions.

Intime Lotte

Restaurants

1 Susu
MAP M2 ▪ 10 Qiangliang Xixiang, off Qianliang Hutong ▪ 8400 2699 ▪ ¥¥

Susu serves light Vietnamese fare, including spring rolls. The English-speaking staff can turn meat dishes into vegetarian options. Book ahead.

2 Dong Lai Shun
MAP N4 ▪ 198 Wangfujing Dajie ▪ 6513 9661 ▪ ¥¥

An old name well-known for Mongolian-style hot pots. Get plates of sliced meat and vegetables to cook your own meal in a copper-funneled pot.

Oriental Plaza Food Court

3 Oriental Plaza Food Court
MAP N4 ▪ Corner of Dong Chang'an Jie and Wangfujing Dajie ▪ ¥

The basement of this upscale shopping mall has a Southeast Asian-style food court offering everything from good Chinese street food to sushi.

4 Made In China
MAP N5 ▪ Grand Hyatt, 1 Dong Chang'an Jie ▪ 6510 9608 ▪ ¥¥¥

A classy venture with stunning design and even better food.

5 Jing
MAP N4 ▪ The Peninsula Beijing Hotel, 8 Jinyu Hutong ▪ 6510 6714 ▪ Open 5:30–11:30pm daily ▪ ¥¥¥

Enjoy an outstanding Asian-flavored fusion menu in refined surrounds.

6 TRB Bites
95 Donghuamen Dajie, Dongcheng District ▪ ¥¥¥

One of Beijing's top restaurants shows its more casual side, but its pedigree shines through. Choose from around 20 selections to customize your three to five courses.

7 Haidilao Hot Pot
MAP N4 ▪ 8th Floor, Tianyingtai Department Store, 88 Wangfujing Dajie ▪ 5762 0153 ▪ Open 24/7 ▪ ¥

Try hand-pulled noodles and play board games, get your shoes shined, or have a manicure while you wait.

8 Quanjude
MAP N5 ▪ 9 Shuai Fu Yuan Hutong, Wangfujing Dajie ▪ 6302 3062 ▪ Closes at 9pm ▪ ¥¥

Beijing's most famous duck restaurant has several branches but this is definitely the most convenient, just a short walk from southern Wangfujing.

9 Tianjin Bai Jiaoyuan
12 Xinwenhua Jie, Xicheng District ▪ 6605 9371 ▪ ¥

Loosely translated as "100 dumplings," and hailing from the neighboring city of Tianjin, this spot is known for its incredible variety of fillings and dumpling skin colors.

10 Huang Ting
MAP N4 ▪ The Peninsula Beijing Hotel, 8 Jinyu Hutong ▪ 8516 2888 ▪ ¥¥

Enjoy Cantonese cuisine amid splendid antique furniture in the basement of a five-star hotel.

See map on pp68–9

TOP 10 South of Tian'an Men Square

The Qian Men (Front Gate) at the southern end of Tian'an Men Square was once part of the inner walls that divided the imperial quarters from the "Chinese city," where the massed populace lived. Walking south from the gate you are plunged into a network of lively *hutongs* (alleys), the remnants of the old quarter. Continuing south down Qian Men Dajie brings you to the western perimeter of the grounds of the Temple of Heaven, one of Beijing's most evocative sights.

Incense burner at Fayuan Temple

① Fayuan Temple
MAP C6 ■ 7 Fayuan Si Qian Jie ■ 6353 4171 ■ Subway: Caishikou, then a 10-minute walk ■ Open 8:30am–3:30pm daily ■ Adm

Dating from AD 696, this is likely the oldest temple in Beijing. Near the gate, the incense burner is flanked by the Drum and Bell Towers. Beyond, the Hall of the Heavenly Kings is guarded by a pair of bronze lions. A hall contains a large statue of Buddha.

SOUTH OF TIAN'AN MEN SQUARE

Colorful building in Liulichang

and musicians, Liulichang takes its name from the glazed tile factory once located here. The streets are lined with shops selling Chinese paintings, musical instruments, porcelain, and calligraphy – look out for the giant ink brushes hanging in the windows. During Chinese New Year, Liulichang is home to one of Beijing's most colorful Temple Fairs.

2 Liulichang
MAP D5 ■ Subway: Heping Men
Head west from the bustle of Qian Men and Dazhalan into a more peaceful *hutong* district. Historically a gathering spot for writers, artists,

3 Qian Men and Dazhalan
MAP D5–E5 ■ Subway: Qian Men
A historical royal street as well as a traditional shopping area, Qian Men Dajie has been redeveloped into a period-themed shopping boulevard replete with a faux-1920s tram and birdcage-like streetlamps. Running east and west off the northern end of Qian Men is Dazhalan Jie, or Dashilan, an old *hutong* area that can be explored on foot or by rickshaw. It is full of Qing-era specialty shops selling pickles, tea, silks, as well as traditional Chinese medicine.

4 Beijing Planning Exhibition Hall
MAP L6 ■ 20 Qian Men Dong Dajie ■ 6701 7074 ■ Subway: Qian Men ■ Open 9am–5pm Tue–Sun ■ Adm ■ www.bjghzl.com.cn
On display at this four-floor museum are dreams of the architecture and urban landscape of Beijing to be. These are dramatically represented through film and interactive exhibits, plus a vast model that covers most of the third floor. An interesting section is dedicated to Beijing's urban makeover for the 2008 Olympics.

Beijing Planning Exhibition Hall

5 Legation Quarter
MAP M5 ▪ Subway: Qian Men

At the end of the Second Opium War, in 1860, foreign delegations were permitted to take up residence in a quarter southeast of the Forbidden City. On Dong Jiao Min Xiang and the surrounding streets, the first modern foreign buildings in Beijing took root. The embassies have long since left, and new occupants have moved in. The former American legation, for instance, is now a bar, restaurant, and lifestyle complex. Also here are the former City Bank of New York, now the Beijing Police Museum (see p40), and St. Michael's Church (see p43).

THE BOXERS

The Boxers, a band of xenophobic rebels from north China who rose up to rid China of the "foreign devils," drew from superstitious rituals that they believed made them invulnerable. Supported by the Empress Dowager Cixi (see p29), the rebels laid waste to Beijing's Legation Quarter in 1900 while besieging the district's foreign population. The siege was eventually broken by an eight-power allied force.

6 Temple of Heaven

The name refers to a vast complex that encompasses a large, marble sacrificial altar, the iconic three-story Hall of Prayer for Good Harvests, the smaller Imperial Vault of Heaven, and many ancillary buildings, all set in a landscaped park. Allow at least a half-day to take in everything (see pp16–17).

Ornate hall in the Temple of Heaven

Looking inside Niu Jie Mosque

7 Niu Jie Mosque
MAP C6 ▪ 88 Niu Jie ▪ 6353 2564 ▪ Subway: Guanganmennei, then walk ▪ Open 8am–sunset daily ▪ Adm

Beijing's oldest and largest mosque dates back to the 10th century. It's an attractive building with Islamic motifs and Arabic verses decorating its halls. Astronomical observations were made from the tower-like Wangyue Lou. The lush courtyard is an idyllic escape from the city streets. Visitors should dress conservatively, and non-Muslims are not allowed to enter the prayer hall.

8 South Cathedral
MAP J6 ▪ 141 Qian Men Xi Dajie ▪ Subway: Xuanwu Men

The first Catholic church to be built in Beijing stands on the site of the residence of the first Jesuit missionary to reach the city, Matteo Ricci. Arriving in 1601, the Italian won the favor of the Wanli emperor by presenting him with gifts of European curiosities such as mathematical instruments and clocks. Ricci founded the church in 1605, although the present building dates to 1904, replacing a structure that was burned down during the Boxer Rebellion. It has some fine stained-glass windows.

9 Natural History Museum
MAP E6 ▪ 126 Tangqiao Nan Dajie ▪ 6702 7702 ▪ Subway: Zhushikou, then walk ▪ Open 8:30am–5pm Tue–Sun ▪ www.bmnh.org.cn

An overbearing piece of 1950s architecture houses a great collection of dinosaur skeletons, as well as stuffed pandas and other animals. There are also fish, both dead (preserved in formaldehyde) and alive (in the aquarium). Visitors of a nervous disposition may want to skip the partially dissected human cadavers up on the third floor.

Ancient Architecture Museum

10 Ancient Architecture Museum
MAP D6 ▪ 21 Dongjing Lu ▪ 6304 5608 ▪ Bus 15 to Nanwei Lu ▪ Open 9am–4pm Tue–Sun ▪ Adm

Housed in the Hall of Jupiter, part of the Xianong Tan temple complex, this museum focuses on the ancient construction techniques of Beijing buildings, all helpfully illuminated with detailed models. A fascinating three-dimensional plan shows the city as it was in 1949, its city walls and gates largely intact.

A DAY SOUTH OF TIAN'AN MEN SQUARE

Tian'an Men Square
Legation Quarter
Old Qian Men Railway Station
Police Museum
Beijing Planning Exhibition Hall
Southern Fish
Tongrentang Pharmacy
Liubiju
Ruifuxiang
Deyuan
Spoonful of Sugar
Dazhalan Jie

▶ MORNING

Start on Tian'an Men Square, at the southeast corner beside the stripey brick **Old Qian Men Railway Station**, built by the British in 1906, partly to bring military forces straight to the assistance of foreigners in the event of a repeat of the siege of the Boxers. It's now a Railway Museum *(see p18)*. Venture east along Dong Jiao Min Xiang into the **Legation Quarter** to visit the Police Museum *(see p40)*. On leaving, head south to Qian Men Dong Dajie and walk back west for a glimpse of the Beijing of the future at the **Beijing Planning Exhibition Hall** *(see p75)*. From the museum, head into the *hutongs* toward Dazhalan for some crispy roast duck at **Deyuan** *(see p79)*.

AFTERNOON

Head east along **Dazhalan Jie** *(see p75)*. This is a great place for specialty shops. Located down the first alley is 400-year-old **Liubiju** *(see p78)*, selling a vast array of pickles. **Ruifuxiang** *(see p78)* dates from 1893 and is renowned for silks. **Tongrentang Pharmacy** *(see p78)* has been in business since 1669, while **Zhangyiyuan Chazhuang** has been trading teas since the early 20th century. Then, after all that tea, head back west to **Spoonful of Sugar** *(see p79)* for a coffee break, then grab a spicy Hunan dinner at **Southern Fish** *(see p79)*.

See map on pp74–5 ←

Shops

Souvenir shop on Liulichang

1 Liulichang
This picturesque street was renovated in the 1980s to give it an Old China look. It's still fun to browse for antiques and art supplies (see p75).

2 Hong Qiao Market
MAP F6 ■ 36 Hong Qiao Lu ■ Open 10am–7pm daily
Specializing in pearls and precious stones, this indoor market also sells clothes, bags, and shoes (see p60).

3 Panjiayuan Antique Market
MAP E5 ■ Panjiayuan Qiao ■ 6775 2405 ■ Subway: Panjiayuan ■ Open 8:30am–6pm Mon–Fri, 4:30am–6pm Sat & Sun
Set the alarm for dawn for a treasure hunt down at Beijing's sprawling flea market (see p61).

Panjiayuan Antique Market

4 Beijing Curio City
MAP E5 ■ 21 Dong San Huan Nan Lu ■ 6774 7711 ■ Subway: Panjiayuan ■ Open 10am–7pm daily
Just south of Panjiayuan, Curio City has four levels of antiques, porcelain, carpets, Buddhist statues and jewelry.

5 Neiliansheng
MAP E5 ■ 34 Dazhalan Jie ■ 6301 4863
Beijing's best-known shoe store, in business since 1853 is known for supplying footwear to Chairman Mao.

6 Maliandao Tea Market
MAP B6 ■ 11 Maliandao Lu, Guang'anmen Wai ■ Bus 46, 89, 414, or special line 27 ■ Open 9am–7pm daily
This three-floor market (literally, "tea street") could also be called "Little Fujian," so ubiquitous are traders from China's tea capital. It's Beijing's best place to buy or sample an incredible variety of teas.

7 Ruifuxiang
MAP E5 ■ 5 Dazhalan Dong Jie ■ 6303 5313 ■ Open 9am–9pm daily
Silk has been sold on this precise spot since 1893. Tailors can create pretty blouses and qipaos (the old-style Chinese dress).

8 Beijing Silk Store
MAP E5 ■ Zhubao Shi 5 ■ 6301 6658
This venerable store is said to date back to 1840. Prices for quality tailoring and ready-made clothes are reasonable.

9 Tongrentang Pharmacy
MAP E5 ■ 24 Qian Men Dazhalan
Founded in 1669, Tongrentang is China's oldest pharmacy. The store stocks thousands of traditional medicines, some of which were used in the imperial court.

10 Liubiju
MAP E5 ■ 3 Liangshidian Jie
A jar of Chinese pickles may not be high on your list of essentials but a visit to this colorful, 400-year-old shop should be.

→ *See map on pp74–5*

Restaurants and Teahouses

PRICE CATEGORIES
For the equivalent of a meal for two made up of a range of dishes, served with two glasses of wine, and including service.

¥ under ¥250   ¥¥ ¥250–¥500
¥¥¥ over ¥500

1 Soloist Coffee Co
MAP E5 ■ 39 Yangmeizhu Xiejie, near Maishi Jie ■ 5711 1717 ■ ¥
Soloist's coffee is roasted in-house, and wait staff are friendly coffee snobs who make perfect brews.

2 Lao She Teahouse
MAP L6 ■ 3 Qian Men Xi Dajie ■ 6303 6830 ■ www.laoshe teahouse.com ■ ¥¥
One of the first in a renaissance of old-style Beijing teahouses. Opera and acrobatics shows take place in a small upstairs theater.

3 Liqun Roast Duck Restaurant
MAP M6 ■ 11 Beixianfeng Hutong, enter via Zhengyi Lu ■ 6702 5681 ■ ¥¥
Beijing duck at this little courtyard restaurant is usually sublime, despite the rough-and-ready ambience.

4 Capital M
MAP L6 ■ 3/F, 2 Qian Men Dajie ■ 6702 2727 ■ ¥¥¥
With a splendid view across Tian'an Men Square, Australian restaurateur Michelle Garnault's Beijing outpost serves innovative international cuisine.

Vast dining room at Capital M

5 Qian Men Quanjude
MAP L6 ■ 32 Qian Men Dajie ■ 6511 2418 ■ ¥¥
The most famous of the Quanjude restaurants and the worse for it. But call by for take-away duck pancakes.

6 Southern Fish
166 Yang Mei Zhu Xie Jie ■ ¥¥
In the heart of the *hutongs* lies this popular place with only nine tables serving spicy Hunan classics. Book ahead or take your chances *(see p57)*.

7 Spoonful of Sugar
59 Tieshuxie Jie, Xicheng District ■ 6308 3971 ■ Closed Mon ■ ¥
A creative café menu includes chicken sandwiches with glazed onions and garlic mushrooms.

8 Deyuan
MAP E5 ■ 57 Dashilan Xi Dajie, Xicheng District ■ 6308 5371 ■ ¥¥
One of the better places to enjoy duck with locals, not tourists – and at bargain prices, too.

9 Lost Heaven
MAP E4 ■ 23 Chien Men Qian Men Dong Dajie ■ 8516 2698 ■ ¥¥¥
A luxuriously designed restaurant serving a tangy fusion of Yunnan, Thai, and Burmese cuisines.

10 Lao Beijing Zhajiang Mian Da Wang
MAP E5 ■ 56 Dong Xinglong Jie ■ 6705 6705 ■ ¥
A bustling eatery selling traditional Beijing snacks. Cheap and tasty fare.

🔟 North of the Forbidden City

An almost contiguous run of lakes, either set in parkland or surrounded by charming *hutongs*, stretches through the neighborhood north of the Forbidden City. It's a rewarding area to explore on foot: along its narrow streets you'll find ancient temples and grand old courtyard residences, and the recent influx of restaurants, bars, and shops has not spoiled the picturesque setting.

Boating in Bei Hai Park

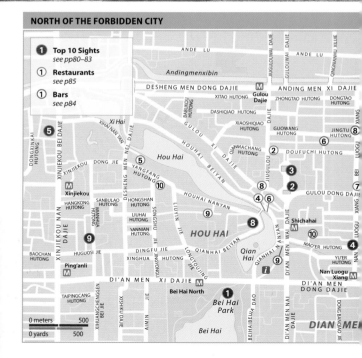

NORTH OF THE FORBIDDEN CITY

1	**Top 10 Sights** see pp80–83
①	**Restaurants** see p85
①	**Bars** see p84

1 Bei Hai Park

A classic imperial garden, Bei Hai was a summer playground for successive dynasties that ruled from the neighboring Forbidden City. Now open to the public, it is thronged by locals who come here to socialize. There are a couple of small temples, a fine, small ornamental garden, and a noted restaurant. This is arguably the loveliest of Beijing's many fine city parks (see pp24–5).

2 Drum Tower

MAP E2 ■ Gulou Dong Dajie ■ 8403 6706 ■ Subway: Shichahai ■ Open 9am–5:30pm daily ■ Adm

Drum towers (gu lou) were once found in all major Chinese towns. They housed large drums that were beaten to mark the hour, keeping the city's civil servants on time for work. This structure dates to 1420. Visitors can clamber up the steep steps to inspect some 25 drums and be

Inside the 15th-century Drum Tower

entertained by drummers delivering skin-thumping performances. Call ahead for performance times.

3 Bell Tower

MAP E1 ■ Gulou Dong Dajie ■ 8403 6706 ■ Subway: Shichahai ■ Open 9am–5:30pm daily ■ Adm

Dating from 1745, this replaces an earlier tower that burned down. The heavy bell it contains used to be rung to mark the closing of the city gates in the evening. During Spring Festival visitors are allowed to ring the bell for a donation of ¥100. The views from both the Drum and Bell Towers over the neighboring hutongs are well worth the exhausting climb.

4 Nan Luogu Xiang

MAP E2

Less than 10 minutes' walk east of the Drum Tower, Nan Luogu Xiang is arguably Beijing's hippest hutong. Still traditional in feel, the alley is home to a few small hotels, several interesting clothing and craft boutiques, and a number of cafés and bars. Baochao Hutong, nearby, is a hipster hangout that's popular with the locals.

Boutique in Nan Luogu Xiang

5 Xu Beihong Memorial Museum

MAP D1 ■ 53 Xinjiekou Bei Dajie ■ 6225 2187 ■ Subway: Jishuitan ■ Open 9am–4pm Tue–Sun ■ Adm (audio guide ¥10, plus ¥100 deposit)

Set back from the road with a sign on top in green characters, this museum is dedicated to the man regarded as the founder of modern Chinese painting. It exhibits a collection of the lively watercolors of horses that made Xu Beihong (1885–1953) internationally famous.

Statue at the Confucius Temple

6 Lama Temple (Yonghe Gong)

About a 30-minute walk east of the Drum and Bell Towers, or just a few minutes south of the Yonghe Gong subway station, the Lama Temple is Beijing's largest working temple complex. It is filled every day with about an equal number of worshipers and visitors (see pp20–21).

7 Confucius Temple (Kong Miao)

MAP F1 ■ 13 Guozi Jian Jie ■ 8402 7224 ■ Subway: Yonghe Gong ■ Open 8:30am–4:30pm daily ■ Adm

Just west of the Lama Temple, the Confucius Temple was built in 1302 during the Mongol Yuan dynasty, and expanded in 1906. Around 200 ancient stelae stand in the courtyard in front of the main hall, inscribed with the names of those who successfully passed the imperial civil service exams. On a marble terrace inside the hall are statues of Confucius and some of his disciples.

8 Hou Hai

The most visitor-friendly neighborhood of Beijing, Hou Hai consists of three joined lakes surrounded by an expansive and labyrinthine sprawl of age-old

Red-and-gold pavilion at the Lama Temple (Yonghegong)

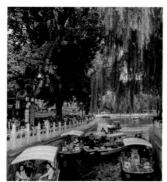

Willow-lined lake in Hou Hai

hutongs (alleys). Visit to admire a handful of well-preserved mansions, as well as for the opportunity to see a more humble form of Beijing life as it has been lived for centuries (see pp26–7).

9 Former Residence of Mei Lanfang

MAP D2 ■ 9 Huguosi Jie ■ 8322 3598 ■ Subway: Jishuitan ■ Open 9am–4pm Tue–Sun ■ Adm ■ www. meilanfang.com.cn

This was the home of Beijing Opera's greatest ever performer (1894–1961). The rear rooms have been left with their traditional furniture as it was when he died. Others contain a hagiographic account of his life, as well as diagrams of the stylized movements required by the form, and a video of Mei, aged 61 but still playing the young girl roles for which he was famous (see p52).

10 Di Tan Park

MAP F1 ■ North of Lama Temple ■ Subway: Yonghe Gong ■ Open 6am–9pm daily ■ Adm ■ www.dtpark.com

The park was named for the Altar of Earth (Di Tan), which was a venue for imperial sacrifices. The altar's square shape represents the earth. These days, the park is always full of pensioners strolling, chatting, and exercising. A lively temple fair is held here at Chinese New Year.

A DAY IN THE HUTONGS

▶ MORNING

Take an early morning stroll along **Wudingyao Hutong**, where you can have breakfast at one of the cafés. Then continue on to the **Lama Temple** (see pp20–21). On leaving, cross over the main road and pass under the *pailou* (gate) at the entrance to Guozi Jian Jie for the **Confucius Temple**. Afterward, sample Guozi Jian's many cafés, or browse through the city's best traditional craft shops. At the western end of Guozi Jian Jie turn left onto **Anding Men Nei** Dajie, a wide, shop-filled avenue, follow it south across Jiaodaokuo Dong Dajie and take a right on Dongmianhua Hutong, one of the more vibrant of the city's old alleys. Take the first left onto **Nan Luogu Xiang** (see p81), cross Gu Lou Dong Dajie to **Bei Luogu Xiang**, and stop for a Yunnan lunch on the terrace of **Yun'er Small Town** (see p85) before hitting the boutiques.

AFTERNOON

Head west along **Mao'er Hutong** until you reach **Di'an Men Wai Dajie**, where you turn right and up the street for the **Drum and Bell Towers** (see p81). Climb the towers to see the route you've just taken. Retrace your steps back down Di'an Men Wai Dajie taking the very first right, a tiny opening (usually marked by waiting taxis) leading into **Yandai Xie Jie**. At the end of this crooked alley is the **Silver Ingot Bridge**; cross and bear left for **Lotus Lane**. For dinner, head east back into the *hutongs* for a cozy Italian meal at **Mercante** (see p57).

See map on pp80–81

Bars

The Distillery by Capital Spirits

1 Cuju
MAP F2 ∎ 28 Xiguan Hutong
∎ 6407 9782

This tiny, cube-shaped bar has TV screens for watching soccer. It serves great Moroccan street food, and a selection of uniquely infused rums.

2 The Distillery by Capital Spirits
MAP F2 ∎ 23 Xinsi Hutong ∎ 6409 3319

With a stripped-down bar and a cozy lounge, this remodeled traditional *siheyuan* offers great views. Try the house gin or vodka, fresh from the copper still on site.

3 Ramo
MAP F1 ∎ 64 Fangjia Hutong
∎ 8403 5004

A casual bar with minimalist, polished-concrete decor, this place is often filled with young foreign residents. It serves a variety of imported ales and snacks.

4 Mao Mao Chong
MAP E2 ∎ 12 Banchang Hutong, off Jiaodaokou Nanje ∎ 158 4271 9052

This classy and affordable *hutong* bar offers a selection of creative cocktails, plus gourmet pizzas – with a special offer available every Tuesday.

5 The Tiki Bungalow
MAP F2 ∎ 34 Jiaodaokou Bei Santiao

This roomy, popular *hutong* bar brings the tropics to Beijing. There are over 60 cocktails, and the staff have an intimate knowledge of rum.

6 Modernista
MAP E1 ∎ 44 Baochao Hutong ∎ 136 9142 5744

Keep the winter chill at bay with the delicious warm wine served at this 1920s-themed jazz and piano bar. In summer, try their sangria *(see p59)*.

7 Capital Spirits
MAP F2 ∎ 3 Daju Hutong
∎ 6409 3319

China's national alcohol, *baiju*, is often compared to paint thinner. However, if you still want to try it, this is the place. Call to be let in.

8 Mai
MAP E1 ∎ 40 Bei Luogu Xiang
∎ 138 1125 2641

Visit this tiny bar to choose from a wide range of cocktails prepared by a trained mixologist *(see p58)*.

9 East Shore Live Jazz Café
MAP E2 ∎ 2 Qianhai Nanyan Lu
∎ 8403 2131

Opened by famous jazzman Liu Yuan, this bar has steep wooden stairs, four walls of floor-to-ceiling windows and a roof terrace, plus live music.

10 Great Leap Brewery
MAP E2 ∎ 6 Doujiao Hutong, off Di'an Men Wai Dajie ∎ 5717 1399

Located on a quiet *hutong*, this craft beer pioneer offers a pleasant courtyard and comfy sofas.

Restaurants

1 Dali Courtyard
MAP E2 ▪ 67 Xiaojingchang Hutong, Gulou Dong Dajie ▪ 8404 1430 ▪ ¥

Book ahead for the spicy Yunnan dishes at this laid-back restaurant in a beautiful courtyard.

2 Cafe Sambal
MAP E1 ▪ 43 Doufuchi Hutong, off Jiugulou Dajie ▪ 6400 4875 ▪ ¥

An old-style courtyard house serves as the venue for exquisite dishes cooked by a talented and creative Malaysian chef.

3 Café Zarah
MAP E2 ▪ 42 Gulou Dong Dajie ▪ 8403 9807 ▪ ¥

Massive windows and an ultra-modern courtyard make this a place to linger. Coffee and cocktails are the standouts; they also offer light lunches and European breakfasts.

4 Kaorou Ji
MAP E2 ▪ 14 Qianhai Dong Yan ▪ 6404 2554 ▪ ¥

This place majors in Qingzhen – Hui or Muslim – cuisine, which means mutton. The specialty is barbecued lamb and sesame seed bread.

5 Kong Yiji
MAP E2 ▪ Desheng Men Nei Dajie ▪ 6618 4917 ▪ ¥

A lovely lakeside restaurant with a range of exquisite dishes from the Yangzi River delta.

6 Nuage
MAP E2 ▪ 22 Qian Hai Dong Yan ▪ 6401 9581 ▪ ¥

A well-respected Vietnamese restaurant with a lovely location just south of the Silver Ingot Bridge.

7 Yun'er Small Town
MAP E1 ▪ 84 Bei Luogu Xiang ▪ ¥

A cheaper option, Yun'er has a rooftop terrace and the best Yunnan fried cheese in town *(see p57)*.

8 Raj
MAP E1 ▪ 31 Gulou Xi Dajie ▪ 6401 1675 ▪ ¥

Head here for cheap and authentic south Indian cuisine. Decor is kitsch, but there's a pleasant rooftop terrace.

Ganesha statue at Indian eaterie Raj

9 Mei Fu Mei Mansion
MAP D2 ▪ 24 Daxiangfeng Hutong ▪ 6612 6845 ▪ ¥¥¥

This restaurant is set within a gorgeous courtyard house lavishly filled with antiques. Set menus of sweet and rich Shanghainese cuisine are also available.

10 Li Family Imperial Cuisine
MAP D2 ▪ 11 Yangfang Hutong ▪ 6618 0107 ▪ ¥¥¥

Intimate courtyard restaurant serving imperial court cuisine. Set menus are very expensive, but the food is exquisite.

See map on pp80–81

🔟 Eastern Beijing

East of central Beijing, in a corridor between the Second and Third Ring Roads, is the district of Chaoyang. It's not an area that is particularly old and it doesn't have very many significant monuments, but it is home to two main clusters of international embassies, and it is where a large proportion of the city's expatriate community chooses to live. As a result, Chaoyang is the city's entertainment and nightlife center, and, for the visitor, it is the prime area for eating and shopping.

CCTV Tower, Central Business District

EASTERN BEIJING

① Top 10 Sights
see pp88–91

① Restaurants
see p93

① Shops, Markets, and Malls
see p92

Previous pages The Great Wall of China at Jinshanling

to about half of the city's luxury hotels and two of its glitziest shopping malls, China World and Parkview Green (see p92).

Courtyard of the Ancient Observatory

1 Ancient Observatory

MAP G4 ▪ 6524 2202
▪ Subway: Jianguo Men ▪ Open 9am–4pm Tue–Sun ▪ Adm

Dating to 1442, Beijing's observatory is one of the oldest in the world. In fact, there was an even earlier Yuan-dynasty (1279–1368) observatory also located on this site but no trace of that remains. Today, a collection of reproduction astronomical devices lies in the courtyard, some of them decorated with fantastic Chinese designs. There are more impressive instruments on the roof.

2 Central Business District (CBD)

MAP H4 ▪ Subway: Jianguo Men, Yong'an Li, Guomao or Dawanglu

The Central Business District is Beijing's business hub, housing more than 60 percent of the city's foreign-funded companies. Marked by the CCTV Tower in the northeast and by the Twin Towers of the China World Trade Center in the southwest, the area is also home

Shop-lined street in Sanlitun

3 Blue Zoo Beijing

MAP G3 ▪ South gate of Workers' Stadium ▪ 6591 3397 ▪ Subway: Chaoyang Men ▪ Open 8:30am–7:30pm daily ▪ Adm; children under 3 ft (1 m) free ▪ www.bluezoo.com.cn

Not a zoo at all, but a modern aquarium, reckoned to be the best of its kind in Asia. The main attraction is a central tank holding thousands of fish, plus there are also 18 additional tanks with specifically themed displays (see p49).

4 Sanlitun

MAP H2 ▪ Subway: Tuanjiehu

Beijing's main expat-friendly shopping, dining, and drinking district is centered around Taikoo Li and Nali Patio on Sanlitun Bei Lu, and around the Workers' Stadium on Gongren Tiyuchang Bei Lu. It has a high concentration of international restaurants (see p93) and lots of boutique shopping (see p92). Streets around here, although modern, are tree-lined and, with plenty of cafés for refreshment stops, it is a very pleasant district to wander in.

5 Southeast Corner Watchtower (Dong Bian Men)

MAP G5 ■ South of Jianguo Men Nei Dajie ■ 8512 1554 ■ Subway: Jianguo Men ■ Open 8am–5:30pm daily ■ Adm

Just south of the Second Ring Road, a chunk of the old city wall survives, including the 15th-century Dong Bian Men watchtower. Visitors can climb onto the battlements and walk along a stretch of wall. The tower also houses the Red Gate Gallery art venue.

Southeast Corner Watchtower

6 Laitai Flower Market

9 Maizidian Xi Lu, Chaoyang District ■ 6463 5588 ■ Open 9am–5:30pm daily (to 6pm Fri–Sun)

This massive glass-fronted building flanked by stone elephants is much more than a flower market. Wander the jungle-like rows, or browse shops for quirky furniture, ceramics, cut bamboo, decorative boxes, and even tropical fish. Wear layers – it can get steamy in here.

7 Ghost Street

MAP F2 ■ Subway: Beixingqiao

Gui Jie, or Ghost Street, is a 1-mile (2-km) stretch of Dong Zhi Men Nei Dajie that come nightfall is jammed with cars double-parked outside its 100 or so restaurants, many of which open 24 hours. The air smells like Sichuan peppercorn and chilies while most establishments favor corny, old-China decor with plenty

ALTARED CITY

Ri Tan Park's Altar of the Sun is one of eight such cosmologically aligned structures, along with the Altar of Heaven (Tian Tan; see pp16–17), the Altar of Agriculture (Xiannong Tan; now part of the Ancient Architecture Museum; see p77), the Altar of the Moon in the west of the city, the Altar of Earth (Di Tan, see p83), the Altar of the Country in Zhong Shan Park, the Altar of the Silkworm in Bei Hai Park, and the lost Altar of the Gods of Heaven.

of red lacquer and pagoda motifs, and waitresses in silk tunics. This is the home of one of the most popular dishes in Beijing: the hot pot, although all regional Chinese cuisines are represented here.

8 Workers' Stadium

MAP G2 ■ Gongren Tiyuchang Bei Lu ■ 6501 6655 ■ Subway: Dong Si Shi Tiao

With an estimated capacity of 72,000, the stadium is home to Beijing's premier soccer club, Beijing Guo'an, and it is the city's main venue for large-scale rock and pop concerts. Perplexingly, it is also a hub of Beijing nightlife, with numerous clubs and bars clustered around its north and west gates, and some very good restaurants too. Even oldies get in on the act, with mass open-air dancing taking place on the forecourt of the north gate most summer evenings.

9 Dong Yue Miao

MAP G3 ■ 141 Chaoyang Men Wai Dajie ■ 6551 0151 ■ Subway: Chaoyang Men ■ Open 8:30am–4:30pm Tue–Sun ■ Adm

This colorful, active temple dating to the early 14th century is tended by Daoist monks. The main courtyard leads into the Hall of Tai Shan, with statues of gods and their attendants.

Statues in the Dong Yue Miao temple

10 Ri Tan Park

MAP G4 ■ Guanghua Lu ■ 8561 6301 ■ Subway: Jianguo Men ■ Open 6:30am–9:30pm daily

One of the city's oldest parks, Ri Tan was laid out around a sacrificial altar in the 16th century. The round altar remains, ringed by a wall, but this is very much a living park, filled daily with people walking and exercising. The park is well maintained and is surrounded by restaurants and cafés.

Red lanterns hanging in Ri Tan Park

A WALK FROM RI TAN PARK TO SANLITUN

▶ MORNING

Start the day at the **Southeast Corner Watchtower**, for an aerial view from one of Beijing's last remaining city walls. Browse the **Red Gate Gallery** for some of the best in Chinese contemporary art, then walk to the **Ancient Observatory** (see p89) to see ancient brass instruments (and another rooftop view). Keep heading north, but take a break in **Ri Tan Park**, one of the city's more picturesque green spots. The park is home to a lake and the ruins of a sacrificial altar, but it is better known for the countless locals who come to exercise, fly kites, do morning tai chi, or just enjoy the view.

AFTERNOON

Head out of the park via the eastern exit and grab lunch at one of **Ri Tan Lu's** many cafés before continuing north to the vibrant **Dong Yue Miao** temple. Go to the south gate of the **Workers' Stadium** to visit the popular **Blue Zoo Beijing** (see p89), then keep heading north into **Sanlitun** (see p89) for an afternoon of shopping at Taikoo Li. Check out the best Chinese designers at **BNC**, pick up some chic ceramics at **Spin** (for both, see p92), and restock your coffee-table books at **Bookworm** (see p113). For cheap eats, try the **Taco Bar**, or go to **Jing Yaa Tang** (for both, see p93) for something more upmarket. Enjoy a nightcap at **La Social** or **Hidden House** before going dancing on **Migas'** terrace (for all, see p58).

See map on p88

Shops, Markets, and Malls

1 Tailor Shops in Sanlitun
MAP H2 ■ Yashow's side streets (off Gongtibeilu) and Sanlitun Xijie

The streets to the west of Taikoo Li are full of custom tailors who can accommodate your schedule.

Silk Market artist and shopkeeper

2 Silk Market
MAP G4 ■ Jianguo Men Wai Dajie ■ 5169 9003

This four-story market is the place to get silk goods, such as ties, table-cloths, traditional clothes and dressing gowns. It is also filled with counterfeit designer goods (see p61).

3 China World Shopping Mall
MAP H4 ■ 1 Jianguo Men Wai Dajie ■ 6505 2288

The Silk Market sells the counterfeits, but this elegant shopping mall is where you come for the originals.

4 Shin Kong Place
87 Jianguo Lu ■ 6530 5888

Opened in April 2007, Shin Kong is a temple for luxury shopping and gourmet dining. It also marked the debut appearance of many elite brands in mainland China.

5 Sanlitun SOHO
MAP H2 ■ South side of Gongren Tiyuchang Bei Lu ■ 5878 8888

Characterized by some colorful funnel-shaped buildings, Sanlitun SOHO is a vast complex of shopping malls, offices, hotels, and private apartments. Numerous brand stores, banks, restaurants, and cafés occupy the first floor.

6 Brand New China (BNC)
MAP H2 ■ NLG-09a, B1, Sanlitun Village North, 11 Sanlitun Lu ■ 6416 9045

Created by media celebrity Hung Huang, BNC celebrates Chinese fashion. Collect emerging designers' works while they're still affordable.

7 Parkview Green
MAP H4 ■ 9 Dongdaqiao Lu ■ 5690 7000

Chic, eco-friendly mall with a range of fashion wear and accessories – from women's lines by LA-based designer Tadashi Shoji to handmade men's shoes by O'Quirey, plus displays of contemporary art and Salvador Dalí sculptures.

8 Spin
6 Fangyuan Xi Lu, Chaoyang District ■ 6437 8649

These stylish ceramics are more affordable here than in Spin's other bases in Shanghai and New York. Check out the "Seven Fortune" pots.

9 Taikoo Li Sanlitun
MAP H2 ■ 6 Gongren Tiyuchang Bei Lu (corner Sanlitun Bei Lu) ■ 6417 6110

The upscale Village has many brand stores including Apple and Adidas, plus a range of restaurants and bars.

10 Jenny Lou's
MAP G3 ■ 4 Ri Tan Bei Lu ■ 8563 0626

Expat heaven, with Dutch cheese, German bread, and French wines.

Restaurants

1 Jing Yaa Tang
MAP H2 ▪ 1/F The Opposite House Hotel, 11 Sanlitun Bei Lu ▪ 6410 5230 ▪ ¥¥¥
This elegant restaurant specializes in Beijing roast duck and regional Chinese dishes such as Kung Pao chicken and Dandan noodles.

2 Taco Bar
MAP H2 ▪ Unit 10, Electrical Research Institute, Gongti Bei Lu ▪ 6501 6026 ▪ Closed Mon & lunch Tue–Fri ▪ ¥
Warning: the fish tacos here are addictive. Add a pitcher of margarita, and you'll never want to leave. And the price can't be beat.

3 Crescent Moon
MAP F2 ▪ 16 Dong Si Liu Tiao ▪ 6400 5281 ▪ ¥¥
There are no frills here, just great, exotic food served by a team of friendly Uighur waitresses. Don't miss the tasty lamb kebabs.

4 Hatsune
MAP H4 ▪ 2nd floor, Heqiao Building C, 8a Guanghua Dong Lu ▪ 6415 3939 ▪ ¥¥
A class act: this stylish Japanese restaurant has fresh fish flown in daily. The sushi is excellent.

5 Guizhou Luo Luo Suan Tang Yu
MAP F2 ▪ 186 Dong Zhi Men Nei Dajie ▪ 6405 1717 ▪ ¥
"Ghost Street" is always a fun place to dine, and this hot pot specialist is one of its best eateries.

Comfort food at Taco Bar

6 Bottega
MAP H2 ▪ 18 Sanlitun Lu ▪ 6416 1752 ▪ ¥¥
This popular pizzeria also offers pizzas and calzones with charcoal crusts, available for pre-order.

7 Migas
MAP H2 ▪ 6th Floor, Nali Patio, 81 Sanlitun Lu ▪ 5208 6061 ▪ ¥¥¥
Known for its rooftop bar and dance patio, Migas serves Spanish sharing plates like salted cod and steamed eggplant, and oxtail in red wine.

8 Transit
MAP H2 ▪ N4-36, 3/F The Village, North Sanlitun Bei Lu ▪ 6417 9090 ▪ ¥¥
Enjoy beautifully spiced Sichuan cuisine at this sophisticated but unpretentious restaurant.

9 Dianke Dianlai
MAP G3 ▪ 8 Dafangjia Hutong, off Chaoyang Men Nan Jie ▪ 6512 0930 ▪ ¥¥
The menu changes daily at this Yunnan courtyard restaurant.

10 Beijing Dadong Roast Duck Restaurant
MAP H2 ▪ Bdg 3, Tuanjiehu Beikou, Dongsanhuan Bei Lu ▪ 6582 2892 ▪ ¥¥
It is the opinion of a great many Beijingers that there is no finer duck than that served here.

Beijing Dadong Roast Duck Restaurant

See map on p88

TOP 10 Western Beijing

Xicheng, meaning "West City," is the central district west of the Forbidden City and the lakes. Beijingers think of this area as a seat of money and learning – both the Financial District and Haidian University are here. Western Beijing is best experienced as a series of half-day expeditions: a visit to the Military Museum with a look at the Millennium Monument afterward, or a trip to the aquarium followed by the Temple of the Five Pagodas. Expect to make liberal use of taxis and the subway.

Gilded bronze statue at the Capital Museum

1 Capital Museum
MAP B4 ■ 16 Fuxing Men Wai Dajie, Xicheng ■ 6337 0491 ■ Subway: Muxidi ■ Open 9am–5pm Tue–Sun ■ www.capitalmuseum.org.cn
The popular Capital Museum celebrates China's civilization in general and Beijing's history in particular. The five-story building is easily recognizable thanks to its huge bronze cylinder. Exhibits include porcelain art, calligraphy, Buddha statues, furniture, and crafts. Reserve online.

WESTERN BEIJING

Top 10 Sights
see pp94–7

Immense reading room in the National Library of China

2 National Library of China

MAP A1 ■ 33 Zhongguancun Nandajie ■ 8854 5426 ■ Subway: National Library ■ Open 9am–9pm Mon–Fri, 9am–5pm Sat & Sun (except pub hols) ■ www.nlc.gov.cn

One of the five biggest libraries in the world, the National Library of China has been expanded to accommodate its collection of approximately 12 million books. The building's floating roof houses the Digital Library. Most books are reference only, but visitors can request a reader's pass.

3 White Cloud Temple

MAP B4 ■ 6 Baiyun Guan Jie, off Lianhuachi Dong Lu ■ 6346 3531 ■ Subway: Nanlishi Lu ■ Open 8:30am–4:30pm daily (Oct 8–Apr: to 4pm) ■ Adm

The first temple on this site was founded in AD 739 and burnt down in 1166. Since that time, it has been repeatedly destroyed and rebuilt. It even survived being used as a factory during the Cultural Revolution. The shrines, pavilions, and courtyards that make up the compound today date mainly from the Ming and Qing dynasties. Monks here are followers of Daoism and sport distinctive top-knots. Each Chinese New Year this is the venue for one of the city's most popular temple fairs, with performers, artisans, and traders.

4 Temple of Heavenly Tranquility (Tianning Si)

MAP B5 ■ Guang'an Men Nanbinhe Lu ■ Subway: Daguanying, then taxi

This temple, built in the 5th century AD, is one of the city's oldest. The striking octagonal pagoda was added in the early 12th century. The bottom of the pagoda is decorated with carved arch patterns, symbolizing Sumeru, the mountain of the gods. Above are 13 levels of eaves, with no doors or windows – the pagoda is without stairs inside or outside and is, in fact, solid.

Temple of Heavenly Tranquility

Brightly colored flower beds in full bloom at Yuyuan Tan Park

5 Yuyuan Tan Park

MAP A3 ■ Xisanhuan Lu ■
Subway: Military Museum ■ Open
Dec–Mar 6:30am–7pm daily; Apr,
May & Sep–Nov 6am–8:30pm; Jun–
Aug 6am– 9:30pm ■ Adm

Lovely Jade Lake Park is at its most
beautiful during cherry-blossom
season. Rent a boat and traverse
the massive lakes, go for a
swim, or grab a snack
from the food stalls and
have a picnic – unusually
for Beijing – on the grass.

6 Military Museum of the Chinese People's Revolution

MAP A4 ■ 9 Fuxing Lu
■ 6686 6244 ■ Subway:
Military Museum ■ Open
8am–5pm daily ■ Adm
(ID required)

Vast halls of Cold War-
era hardware, including

**Statue in Miaoying
Temple White Dagoba**

lots of silvery fighter
planes and tanks,
fill the first floor of this interesting
military museum. Upstairs has
exhibitions on historic conflicts,
including the Opium Wars and Boxer
Rebellion. Unfortunately, there is
little labeling in English. What is not
mentioned is that the museum is
close to the Muxidi intersection,
scene of a massacre of civilians by
the Chinese army during the
democracy protests of 1989.

7 Miaoying Temple White Dagoba (Baita Si)

MAP C3 ■ 171 Fucheng Men Nei Dajie
■ 6616 6099 ■ Subway: Fucheng Men
■ Open 9am–5pm Tue–Sun ■ Adm

Celebrated for its tall, Tibetan-style
white *dagoba* (stupa), this temple
dates to 1271, when Beijing was
under Mongol rule. The temple
is also noted for
its fascinating
collection of
thousands of Tibetan
Buddhist statues.

8 Lu Xun Museum

MAP C3 ■ 19 Gong Men
Kou Er Tiao, off Fucheng Men
Nei Dajie ■ 6616 4168
■ Subway: Fucheng Men
■ Open 9am–4pm Tue–Sun

Lu Xun is regarded as the
father of modern
Chinese literature,
responsible for such

BUDDHISM IN CHINA

Buddhism started in India and probably
came to China along the Silk Road. The
earliest sign of the religion is linked to
the founding of the White Horse Temple
near the old capital of Luoyang in
AD 68. Buddhism surged in popularity
during periods of instability, when
Confucianism's veneration for authority
did not sit well with the populace. It was
eventually adopted by China's rulers.

ground-breaking works as "Diary of a Madman" and "The True Story of Ah Q". This is the house in which he lived from 1924 to 1926. The rooms display artifacts relating to his life and there's also an adjacent exhibition hall with more than 10,000 letters, journals, photographs, and other personal objects.

9 Temple of the Five Pagodas
MAP B1 ▪ 24 Wuta Si Cun ▪ 6217 3836 ▪ Subway: National Museum or Xizhi Men ▪ Open 9am–4:30pm daily ▪ Adm

This temple displays obvious Indian influences. It was built in the early 15th century in honor of an Indian monk who came to China and presented the emperor with five golden Buddhas. The pagodas sport elaborate carvings of curvaceous females, as well as the customary Buddhas. Also here is the Beijing Art Museum of Stone Carvings, with 2,000 decorative stelae.

Close encounters in Beijing Aquarium

10 Beijing Aquarium
MAP B2 ▪ 108 Gao Liang Qiao Xijie ▪ 6217 6655 ▪ Open 9am–5pm daily ▪ Adm ▪ www.bj-sea.com

Located in the northeastern corner of the zoo is this conch shell-shaped building. It's reputedly the largest inland aquarium in the world, with massive tanks containing thousands of weird and wonderful fish, plus a shark tank, coral reefs and an "Amazon rainforest." Both children and adults will love this place.

WAR AND PEACE

MORNING

Even if you're no big fan of mechanized heavy armor, the **Military Museum of the Chinese People's Revolution** is worth a visit. Exhibits begin with the technology that made China one of the world's first military superpowers, including the "Flying Dragon," an early form of missile launcher. One room is devoted to the gifts that have been bestowed on China's army chiefs and leaders, such as a pistol presented to Chairman Mao by Fidel Castro. Mao's limousine is displayed on the first floor, and one hall is devoted to statues and assorted representations of the Communist Party's great and good. It all makes for a fascinating insight into the mentality of late 20th-century China.

AFTERNOON

Leaving the museum, walk west along Fuxing Lu and take the first right. You will see the **Millennium Monument** and, behind it, **Yuyuan Tan Park**, a relaxing place for a stroll. Pick up a snack from one of the vendors here and have a picnic, or head out to **Cuiwei Mudan Yuan** (3rd Floor, Cui Wei Da Sha, 2 Hua Yuan Lu) for hot pot before continuing on Fuxing Men Wai Dajie toward Muxidi and the **Capital Museum** (see p94). Audio self-guided tours in Chinese and English are available at the entrance. Don't miss the Peking Opera exhibition on the top floor, or the short film on Beijing's urban development, screened in the auditorium on the first floor.

See map on p94

🔟 Greater Beijing

Beijing is vast. Although you could spend all your time without ever straying too far from the area around Tian'an Men Square, you would be missing out on a lot. Sights in the northwest of the city include the unmissable Summer Palace, the intoxicating hillside Xiang Shan Park and the haunting ruins of the Yuanming Yuan, or Old Summer Palace. It's worth trying to squeeze all three into one day's sightseeing. For fans of contemporary urban culture, the 798 Art District in Beijing's northeast is a must, and you can drop in on the markets and bars around Sanlitun on the way back into town.

The lakeside Summer Palace

1 Summer Palace

It's only a short bus or taxi ride from Bagou subway station to the unmissable Summer Palace. The grounds are arranged as a microcosm of nature, with hills and water complemented by bridges, temples, and walkways. It manages to be both fanciful and harmonious at the same time (see pp28–9).

GREATER BEIJING

Ruins at Yuanming Yuan (Old Summer Palace)

② Yuanming Yuan (Old Summer Palace)

28 Qinghua Xi Lu ■ 6262 8501 ■ Subway: Yuanming Yuan Park ■ Open 7am–7pm daily ■ Adm

The name Yuanming Yuan can be translated as "Garden of Perfect Brightness." This was the largest and most elaborate of all the summer palaces of the Qing era. It once contained private imperial residences, pleasure pavilions, Buddhist temples, a vast imperial ancestral shrine, and canals and lakes for pleasure boating. The Qianlong emperor even added a group of European-style palaces designed by Jesuit missionary-artists serving in the Qing court. Today, all that's left are graceful ruins after the complex was destroyed during the Second Opium War (1856–60). A small museum displays images and models of the place as it was.

③ Xiang Shan Park

Wofosi Lu ■ 6259 1155 ■ Bus: 331 from Summer Palace or 634 from Xizhi Men ■ Open 6am–6:30pm daily ■ Adm (separate fee for Azure Clouds Temple)

The wooded parkland area, also known as Fragrant Hills Park, is 2 miles (3 km) west of the Summer Palace. It offers fine views from Incense Burner Peak, which is accessible by a chairlift (for a fee). Close to the park's main gate is the Azure Clouds Temple (Biyun Si), guarded by the menacing deities Heng and Ha in the Mountain Gate Hall. A series of halls leads to the Sun Yat Sen Memorial Hall, where the revolutionary leader's coffin was stored in 1925, before being taken to his final resting place in Nanjing.

④ Great Bell Temple (Dazhong Temple)

MAP B1 ■ 31A Beisanhuan Xi Lu ■ 6255 0819 ■ Subway: Dazhongsi ■ Open 8:30am–9:30pm daily ■ Adm

This 18th-century temple follows a typical Buddhist plan, with a Heavenly Kings Hall, Main Hall, and a Guanyin Bodhisattva Hall. What distinguishes it, though, is the massive bell – one of the world's largest – housed in the rear tower. The bell was cast between 1403 and 1424, and Buddhist *sutras* in Chinese and Sanskrit cover its surface.

Ornate bell at the Great Bell Temple

Graffiti art on the wall of an industrial unit in the 798 Art District

5 798 Art District

Although it's called the 798 Art District (known locally as Da Shan Zi), Factory number 798 is only one of the several former industrial units taken over by artists and galleries. The 798 features many of Beijing's best galleries, including UCCA and Pace *(see pp30–31)*.

Lily pond, Beijing Botanical Gardens

6 Beijing Botanical Gardens

6259 1283 ▪ Bus: 331 from Summer Palace or 634 from Xizhi Men ▪ Open 7am–5pm daily ▪ Adm ▪ www.beijingbg.com

About a mile (2 km) northeast of Xiang Shan Park lie these pretty gardens, containing some 3,000 plant species and pleasant walks.

The garden's Sleeping Buddha Temple (Wofo Si) is renowned for its magnificent 15-ft (5-m) bronze statue of a reclining Buddha. China's last emperor, Pu Yi *(see p13)*, ended his days here as a gardener.

7 China National Film Museum

9 Nanying Road, Caochangdi Village, Chaoyang ▪ 8435 5959 ▪ Bus: 418 from Dong Zhi Men ▪ Open 9am–4:30pm Tue–Sun (last adm 3:30pm) ▪ Adm ▪ www.cnfm.org.cn

Reportedly the world's largest, this film museum is housed in a glass-and-steel structure and features 20 exhibition halls, an IMAX theater, a digital projection theater, and several 35mm theaters. Over 100 years of Chinese cinema are represented by 1,500 films and 4,300 stills from the works of 450 film-makers.

CHINA'S PEOPLES

China's 1.35 billion population includes about 55 different ethnic minorities, each with their own languages and, in many cases, distinctive customs. Though rich in culture, and varied, together these ethnic minorities make up only eight percent of the population, with the main group, known as Han Chinese, accounting for the rest.

National Aquatics Center (Water Cube)

This Olympic venue proves there is life after the Games – today, the Water Cube is a popular water park, and it is earmarked to host the 2022 Winter Games' curling events. In this collaboration between Chinese and Australian architects, China drew from the classical mythology tradition of a square earth and round heaven, symbolized here by the angled building and the circular stadium. The Australians designed the bubbles, representing soap lather's natural pattern (see p44).

Science and Technology Museum

 Science and Technology Museum

MAP E1 ■ 1 Beisanhuan Zhong Lu ■ 6237 1177 ■ Subway: Beitucheng ■ Open 9am–4:30pm Tue–Sat ■ Adm ■ www.cstm.org.cn

Exhibits begin with ancient science, highlighting China's "technological pre-eminence in history." The technology comes up to date with Chinese space capsules, robots, and an Astro-vision Theater incorporating state-of-the-art cinematography.

 National Olympic Stadium (Bird's Nest)

Inspired by Chinese ceramics, the design of interlocking steel beams was initially supporting a retractable roof. This was later removed, but what remains is still a stunning structure. Since 2008, the Bird's Nest has hosted everything from auto-racing and soccer matches to pop concerts and a winter carnival (see p44).

GREEN BEIJING

▶ **MORNING**

Be at the East Gate (Dong Men) of the **Summer Palace** (see pp28–9) for 8:30am to beat both the heat (if you are visiting in summer) and the crowds. Make your way along the north shore of Kunming Lake via the **Long Corridor** and ascend **Longevity Hill**. Descend again to the Marble Boat and take a pleasure cruiser across the lake to **South Lake Island**. Cross back to the mainland via the supremely elegant **Seventeen-Arch Bridge**; from here it's a short walk north to exit where you came in at the East Gate. In the car park, pick up a taxi and instruct the driver to take you to **Xiang Shan Gongyuan**, otherwise known as Fragrant Hills Park (see p99). Before you enter, **Sculpting In Time** is a café near the East Gate that does good salads, pastas, and pizza.

AFTERNOON

From the park's East Gate, turn right for the **Temple of Brilliance**, built in 1780 and ransacked by Western troops in 1860 and 1900. Close by is the **Liuli Pagoda**, with bells hanging from its eaves that chime in the breeze. Continue north to pass between two small round lakes linked by a small hump-backed bridge – the whole known as the **Spectacles Lakes**. Beyond is a **chairlift** that takes you up to the top of the "Fragrant Hill." Zigzag back down past many more pavilions to arrive at the **Fragrant Hills Hotel**, designed by Chinese-American architect I. M. Pei, best known for his glass pyramid at the Louvre in Paris and the Suzhou Museum near Shanghai.

See map on pp98–9 ←

⑩ Farther Afield

Beijing has more than enough sights to keep the average visitor busy. However, after traveling all this way, it would be a shame not to grasp the opportunity to get out of the city. Of course, the Great Wall of China is high on the list for any visitor, but beyond the bustle of Beijing there are also ancient temples nestled on green hillsides and the vast necropolis of the Ming emperors. To the southwest is the 300-year-old stone Marco Polo Bridge and neighboring Wanping, a rare surviving example of a walled city. Both are an easy suburban bus ride from Beijing. Alternatively, most hotels organize tours to these sights.

Imposing statuary at the Ming Tombs

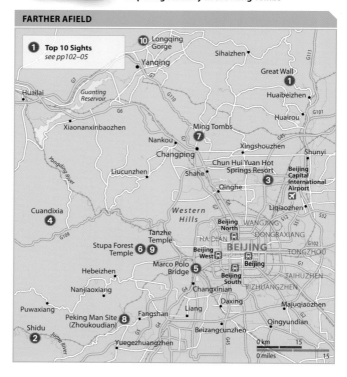

FARTHER AFIELD

① Top 10 Sights
see pp102–05

A stretch of the Great Wall of China surrounded by green hills

1 Great Wall

When in China, a visit to the Great Wall is a must. The closest section to Beijing is at Badaling, and you can get there and back in half a day. However, if you suspect that your appreciation of this matchless monument would be improved by the absence of coach-loads of fellow tourists, then you might want to consider traveling that little bit farther to the sites at Mutianyu, Huanghua Cheng, and Simatai *(see pp34–5)*.

2 Shidu

62 miles (100 km) SW of Beijing ▪ 6134 9009 ▪ Train daily in the late afternoon from Beijing's West Railway station to Shidu

Shidu offers a fabulous escape from the commotion of urban Beijing and a chance to enjoy some stunning natural scenery. Before the new road and bridges were built, travelers had to cross the Juma River ten times as they journeyed through the gorge between Shidu and nearby Zhangfang village, hence the name Shidu, which means "Ten Crossings." Pleasant walking trails wind along the riverbank between impressive gorges and limestone formations.

3 Chun Hui Yuan Hot Springs Resort

20 miles (33 km) N of Beijing ▪ Bus 942 from Dong Zhi Men to Yu Zhuang; from the stop, turn left and walk just over 1 mile (2 km) to the resort, or take a taxi from Beijing ▪ www.chunhuiyuan.cn

After a day of hiking or rock climbing, unwind at the Chun Hui Yuan Hot Springs Resort. Sink into a hot tub, swim in the pool, try a sauna, or book a spa treatment. Everything here is geared toward total rejuvenation.

Boating at the gorge in Shidu

The mountainside village of Cuandixia

4 Cuandixia

Near Zhaitang town, 56 miles (90 km) W of Beijing ■ 6981 9333 ■ Subway: Pingguo Yuan (1 hr), then taxi, or bus 929 (2.5 hrs, twice daily) ■ Adm

On a steep mountainside, Cuandixia is a picturesque hamlet of courtyard houses (siheyuan), most dating from the Ming and Qing dynasties. A ticket allows access to the entire village, which can be explored in a few hours. The population consists of about 70 people. Those wanting an experience of rural hospitality can arrange accommodations with a local family.

5 Marco Polo Bridge

10 miles (16 km) SW of Beijing ■ Subway: Dawayao, then a short taxi ride ■ Open Apr–Oct: 7am–8pm daily; Nov–Mar: 7am–6pm daily

Straddling the Yongding River near the reconstructed Wanping fortress, this marble bridge was first built during the Jin dynasty in 1189 but was destroyed by a flood. The current structure dates to 1698. The bridge acquired its name when legendary voyager Marco Polo described it in his treatise *The Travels*. The balustrades along the length of the bridge are decorated by more than 400 stone lions, each one just slightly different from all the others. On July 7, 1937, the Japanese Imperial Army and Nationalist Chinese soldiers exchanged fire here, an incident that led to the Japanese occupation of Beijing and war.

6 Stupa Forest Temple

28 miles (45 km) W of Beijing ■ 6086 2505 ■ Subway: Pingguo Yuan (1 hr), then bus 931 or tourist bus 7 ■ Open 8am–5pm daily ■ Adm

Near the parking lot for the Tanzhe Temple is this even more fascinating temple, notable for its collection of brick stupas hidden among the foliage. Every single stupa was constructed in memory of a renowned monk. The towering edifices were built in a variety of designs, and the earliest dates from the Jin dynasty (1115–1234).

7 Ming Tombs

The Ming Tombs (see pp32–3) are the resting place for 13 of the 16 Ming emperors. These are Confucian shrines and follow a standard layout of a main gate leading to a series of courtyards and a main hall, with a "soul tower" and burial mound beyond. The tombs are not as colorful and elaborate as Buddhist and Daoist structures, and only three are open to the public, but the necropolis is a worthwhile stop-off as part of an excursion to the Great Wall.

Bronze statue at the Ming Tombs

Diorama at the Peking Man Site

interesting collection of tools and bone fragments. Peking Man himself is not here – his remains mysteriously disappeared during World War II.

⑨ Tanzhe Temple

28 miles (45 km) W of Beijing ■ 6086 2505 ■ Subway: Pingguo Yuan (1 hr), then bus 931 or tourist bus 7 ■ Open 8am–5pm daily ■ Adm

This enormous temple dates back to the 3rd century AD, when it was known as Jiafu Si. It was later renamed for the adjacent mountain, Tanzhe Shan. It has a splendid mountainside setting, and its halls rise up the steep incline. The temple is especially famous for its ancient trees. There are no restaurants in the area, so bring your own lunch.

⑧ Peking Man Site (Zhoukoudian)

30 miles (48 km) SW of Beijing ■ 6930 1278 ■ Bus 917 from Beijing's Tianqiao station to Fangshan, then taxi ■ Open 8:30am–5pm daily ■ Adm

In the 1920s, archeologists removed from a cave at Zhoukoudian some 40-odd fossilized bones and primitive implements, which they identified as the prehistoric remains of Peking Man. It was thought that this exciting discovery provided the much sought-after link between Neanderthals and modern humans. Designated a UNESCO World Heritage Site, the area is geared toward specialists, although the small museum has an

Colorful model of Longqing Gorge

⑩ Longqing Gorge

25 miles (40 km) NW of Beijing ■ Express bus 919 (5.45am–7pm) from Deshengmen Bus Station; get off at Yanqing Dongguan, then take a taxi to Longqingxia

It may seem hard to believe that landscapes as lush as this can be found just 25 miles (40 km) from the bustle of Beijing. Adventure seekers can go bungee-jumping and zip-lining, while those looking for a more relaxing break can pay a visit to the Diamond Temple or rent a rowboat and paddle to a quiet stretch of gorge.

MARCO POLO

Whether Venetian trader and explorer Marco Polo (1254–1324) ever visited China is much disputed. The book he dictated to a ghost writer, who embroidered it substantially, describes aspects of Far Eastern life in much detail, including paper money, the Grand Canal, the structure of a Mongol army, tigers, and the bridge that now bears his name. *The Travels of Marco Polo*, however, may be based on earlier journeys by his father and uncles, and stories from Arab Silk Road merchants.

See map on p102

Streetsmart

Red lanterns hanging for the New Year's celebrations at Di Tan Park

Getting To and Around Beijing

Arriving by Air

Until the new airport opens in late 2019, **Beijing Capital Airport** remains the best way to enter and leave the city. There are direct links to countless national and international locations with China's flagship carrier, **Air China**, as well as international lines **China Airlines**, **China Eastern**, and **China Southern**, plus numerous local carriers. It's also worth checking on flights to neighboring Tianjin and traveling to Beijing by 40-minute bullet train, which runs every 30 minutes and costs ¥58. Check for flights on **Ctrip** or **Elong**.

A taxi from Capital Airport to central Beijing should be ¥100–150, including the ¥5 toll, depending on your location and traffic. Make sure your driver uses the meter, and have your hotel's name and phone number written in Chinese. It is best to avoid the illegal drivers who approach you in the airport.

A cheaper option, at ¥25, is the **Beijing Airport Express**, a subway line that terminates in Dong Zhi Men. Buy your metro card here (start with ¥50 for a week, which you can then top up as necessary), then transfer to city metro, bus, taxi or san lun che (pedicab). Eight shuttle bus lines also run from early morning to around midnight, and tickets for these cost ¥16.

Arriving by Sea

Beijing is a landlocked city, but you can disembark at **Tianjin Port (Tianjin Xingang)** and take a metro, bus or a taxi (around ¥25) to Tanggu Railway Station for the bullet train.

Arriving by Train

China's extensive train network is an excellent way to travel. Newer trains usually ferry businesspeople back and forth, but the older trains are ideal for families. Bring snacks to share, and you'll enjoy warm, cozy journeys. The hub of the country's travel industry, Beijing offers direct international routes to Moscow, Hanoi, Ulaanbaatar, and Pyongyang from **Beijing Railway Station** (metro line 2), **South Railway Station** (lines 4 and 14), and **West Railway Station** (lines 7 and 9). **North Railway Station** (also called Xizhimen Station, lines 2, 4 and 13) is for domestic travel.

Trains come in an alphabet of classes, from G, the highest-level speed train, with business class and soft sleepers, to K, with hard and soft seats, hard and soft sleepers, and deluxe soft sleepers. The hard sleeper is adequate, but avoid the hard seats. Numbered trains are the slowest and have seats only. Stations are signposted in Chinese and English, but arrive at any station one to two hours early to navigate

the crowds – and never travel during the holiday "golden" weeks, May 1 and October 1.

Arriving by Bus

Dong Zhi Men Station (lines 2 and 13, Beijing Airport Express) is Beijing's main bus station, but local stations are scattered around the city and services reach all over China.

Getting Around by Subway

Beijing now has 19 subway lines, with more on the way. The fare varies with distance, but you can get almost anywhere for ¥4. Buy a Transportation Smart Card from any station for bus (discount) and metro (no discount), and top it up at any counter or machine. The subway is well lit and frequent trains operate between 5am and 11:30pm. There is a teller at each stop who will sell you a ticket if you point to your intended stop on a subway map. A bus and subway schedule is available online. Signs and announcements are in Chinese and English, but street maps are only in Chinese, so ask for an exit letter. Most venues are metro accessible.

Getting Around by Bus

For non-Chinese speakers, buses are harder to navigate, but show the Chinese address to a friendly passenger, and they'll tell you when to alight. Use your metro card or cash; some fares are set fees, and some are charged by distance: ¥2 for the first 10 km (6 miles), with ¥1 added every additional 5 km (3 miles). The **Tour Beijing** and **Beijing Trip** websites have prices and other useful information.

Tickets and Transport Cards

You can purchase a Beijing Transportation Smart Card inside metro stations, bus stations, and some Chinese supermarkets for a ¥20 deposit, then top it up as needed. Unused money can be refunded.

Getting Around by Taxi

Although cabs are comparatively affordable, many Beijing taxi drivers lack city knowledge, or see foreigners as easy marks. Never take an unmetered taxi, and avoid parked cars outside tourist attractions; flag one down instead. Black (illegal) cabs are regular cars marked with a horizontal red windshield light; these are not reliable for price or safety. Uber is difficult unless you read Chinese. Make sure you have the destination written in Chinese, and a phone number to call. Note that taxis don't accept credit cards.

Getting Around by Bicycle

Cycling is the ideal way to see Beijing, particularly the *hutongs* and historical areas. You can borrow a bike from most hostels or rent one from such organizations as **Bike Beijing** or **Bicycle Kingdom**. Using public bikes involves a registration process, but it's a good way to save money.

Inexperienced cyclists should take care: e-bike riders and cyclists don't tend to stop at red lights, and they frequently drive and ride on the wrong side of the road. There are bike lanes every-where, but cars use them as parking lots, which forces the riders into the streets. Neither cyclists nor pedestri-ans look both ways before pulling out or stepping into the road, and zebra crossings are nothing more than asphalt decoration. It's best to try a day or so in the quieter *hutongs* to gauge your comfort level. Once you're out in the city traffic, being a proactive, defensive rider is the best course of action.

DIRECTORY

ARRIVING BY AIR

Air China
📞 4008 100 999
🌐 airchina.com.cn

Beijing Airport Express
🌐 en.bcia.com.cn/traffic/express

Beijing Capital Airport
🌐 en.bcia.com.cn

China Airlines
📞 400 888 6998
🌐 china-airlines.com

China Eastern
📞 95530
🌐 en.ceair.com

China Southern
📞 4006 695 539
🌐 csair.com/en/index.shtml

Ctrip
🌐 ctrip.com

Elong
🌐 elong.com

ARRIVING BY SEA

Tianjin Port (Tianjin Xingang)
📞 (22) 2570 5239
🌐 ptacn.com

ARRIVING BY TRAIN

Beijing Railway Station
📞 5101 9999

North Railway Station
📞 5186 6233

South Railway Station
📞 5183 6272

West Railway Station
📞 6321 6263

ARRIVING BY BUS

Dongzhimen Station
📞 6467 1346

GETTING AROUND BY SUBWAY

Bus and Subway Schedule
🌐 travelchinaguide.com/cityguides/beijing/transportation

GETTING AROUND BY BUS

Beijing Trip
🌐 beijingtrip.com

Tour Beijing
🌐 tour-beijing.com/public_bus

GETTING AROUND BY BICYCLE

Bicycle Kingdom
🌐 bicyclekingdom.com

Bike Beijing
🌐 bikebeijing.com
📞 0652 65857

Practical Information

Passports and Visas

Visa requirements are increasingly stringent. Travelers should have six months' validity on their passports and allow at least one month for the application process. Prepare to pay $45–200, depending on country. Visitors also need to be in possession of a return plane ticket and an accommodation itinerary so if you're visiting friends, book a hostel and cancel later. China offers many countries' citizens a 72-hour transit visa, provided they have an international round-trip ticket. Single-entry visas are valid for three months, double-entry for six months, and multiple-entry for six, 12, or 24 months. It's a good idea to carry your passport everywhere; you will need it to purchase tickets and change money. If you need consular assistance, **Australia, Canada, the United Kingdom,** and **the United States** all have embassies in Beijing. You will also need your passport for entry into all museums in Beijing, including the Forbidden City.

Customs Regulations

Few people are searched upon leaving or entering Beijing, but all bags go through a scanner. At politically sensitive times, books may be examined, and anti-China material will be confiscated. Food, two bottles of liquor, and two cartons of cigarettes can avoid duty, while any personal-use electronics brought into the country must be taken out again. If you are carrying ¥20,000 (or any currency worth $5,000), you must declare it. Antiquities, recreational drugs, protected-species products, and weapons are strictly prohibited; even souvenir knives are confiscated from checked luggage. China has zero drug tolerance; to be safe, bring your physician's prescription with you. The Chinese government has a useful website outlining customs regulations.

Travel Safety Advice

For the latest travel safety advice, check the websites of the **UK Foreign and Commonwealth Office**, the **Australian Department of Foreign Affairs and Trade**, and the **US Department of State**.

Travel Insurance

Travel insurance is vital. Medical care at foreign hospitals costs US-level prices. Most local Chinese hospitals will not take insurance and will require a hefty deposit for more expensive procedures.

Health

Although China doesn't require vaccinations, those spending months traveling around the country should consider the basics. International-standard facilities – such as **Beijing United Family Hospital**, **International SOS**, and **Hong Kong International Medical Clinic** – have English-speaking doctors, but when visiting Chinese hospitals – even **Peking Union Medical College Hospital**'s international department – you may need an interpreter. (Be sure to mention medications, allergies, and family history – not everyone asks.) Pharmacies sell both Western and traditional Chinese medicine. The **International SOS pharmacy** is ideal for buying over-the-counter medicine and getting advice in English; however contact an international hospital for emergencies.

Those concerned about pollution can download an app for hourly reports. Buy a 2.5PM mask and plan indoor activities for bad days. It is safe to brush your teeth with tap water, but always drink bottled water. Western digestive systems can struggle with the oil in Chinese food, so it's a good idea to bring anti-diarrhea medicine.

Personal Security

Beijing is surprisingly safe, but watch your wallet on public transport. Sanlitun's increased police presence has made this once-sketchy area significantly safer. However, scams are rife; look out for the "art students" in Wangfujing who want to practice their English and sell you paintings, or the locals in Tian'an Men Square who invite you to a teahouse – you may be stuck with a $600 bill. Solo female travelers should choose official taxis and a female pedicab driver – and always stay awake.

Emergency Services

There are English lines for emergencies, such as the **Foreign Emergency Services** as well as the Ambulance number, but to save time, ask a local to make the call. However, it can be quicker to take a taxi to the hospital, rather than waiting for an ambulance.

Currency and Banking

The national currency is the *yuan* (¥), also known as *renminbi* or *kuai* (slang). Notes come in ¥1, ¥5, ¥10, ¥20, ¥50, and ¥100 and 1 and 5 *jiao* (slang: *mao*); coins come in 1 and 5 *jiao*, and ¥1. Most banks have 24-hour ATMs that take both international and domestic cards, as well as international credit cards. To change money, try major banks.

Telephone and Internet

Free Wi-Fi is available at most restaurants and cafés; high-end hotels often charge a room-usage fee, but keep public areas open. You'll need a VPN to access Facebook, Google, and most Western sites. Popular ones are Express, Pandapow, and HideMe, but this situation is fluid, so check reviews before leaving and sign up for free trials. WeChat offers free texting, voice messages, and phone and video calls to local and international users. Apple and Google maps should work with a VPN, or try **Ulmon** or **Baidu**.

The best network provider is **China Unicom**.

Purchase a SIM card at the airport or at local shops (you will need a passport), and test it before you go; call 10100 and wait for the prompt to activate international calling – and ask for discount numbers for international calls. You can buy top-ups from phone shops or via WeChat. Make sure your phone will work in China; GSM phones should have 900 and 1800 Mhz frequencies or bands.

Postal Services

Open 9am–5pm daily, **China Post** has several branches in Beijing, though couriers are usually faster. For next-day deliveries within the city, it's a good idea to ask your hotel to arrange a *kuaidi* – this should cost no more than ¥30.

DIRECTORY

PASSPORTS AND VISAS

Australian Embassy
☎ 5140 4111
🌐 china.embassy.gov.au

British Embassy
☎ 5192 4000
🌐 gov.uk/government/world/organisations/british-embassy-beijing

Canadian Embassy
☎ 5139 4000
🌐 beijing.gc.ca

United States Embassy
☎ 8531 3000
🌐 beijing.usembassy.gov

CUSTOMS REGULATIONS

General Administration of Customs PRC
🌐 english.customs.gov.cn

TRAVEL SAFETY ADVICE

Australian Department of Foreign Affairs and Trade
🌐 smartraveller.gov.au
🌐 dfat.gov.au/travel

UK Foreign and Commonwealth Office
🌐 gov.uk/foreign-travel-advice/China

US Department of State
🌐 travel.state.gov

HEALTH

Beijing United Family Hospital
🌐 beijing.ufh.com.cn
☎ 5927 7120

Hong Kong International Medical Clinic, Beijing
🌐 hkclinic.com
☎ 6553 2288 (24 hours)

International SOS
☎ 6462 9112
🌐 internationalsos.com

Peking Union Medical College Hospital
☎ 6915 9180
🌐 pumch.cn

EMERGENCY SERVICES

Ambulance
☎ 999

Foreign Emergency Services
☎ 6525 5486

TELEPHONE AND INTERNET

Baidu
🌐 baidu.com

China Unicom
🌐 chinaunicom.com.cn

Ulmon
🌐 ulmon.com

POSTAL SERVICES

China Post
🌐 english.chinapost.com.cn

Opening Hours

Restaurants are usually open 10am–10pm, but Chinese restaurants often close 2–5pm, except for the 24-hour options on Gui Jie. Many bars serve snacks until 11pm, and convenience stores and street food are always available. Shops, stores, and supermarkets usually stay open 9am–9pm, while banks, post offices, and pharmacies operate 9am–5pm. Museums and attractions are usually open 9am–4:30pm, but some have shorter winter hours, and nearly all are closed on Mondays. For distant or unusual attractions, it is always best to call ahead to confirm opening hours.

Time Difference

Beijing is eight hours ahead of GMT, 13 hours ahead of New York, and two hours behind Sydney. The city does not use Daylight Saving Time.

Electrical Appliances

Electrical current is 220 volts AC, so North Americans should use dual-voltage appliances or a converter. China uses two parallel flat pins, two parallel round pins, or two or three slanted flat pins – and some sockets accept all of these. Buying a universal adapter is advisable.

Press

China Daily and *Global Times* are the best choices for English-language news; try also **Xinhua**, online.

For entertainment, the big four expat magazines are *Time Out Beijing*, *That's Beijing*, and *City Weekend*. For English-language radio and television, try *CRI (China Radio International)*, and *CCTV9* for documentaries and news. CCTV also has channels in Spanish, Russian, French, and Arabic. Big hotels sell magazines such as *Time* and *The Economist*, and offer CCTV, BBC, HBO, and Hong Kong cable.

Driver's License

Foreigners staying for less than three months can apply for a temporary license at **Beijing Capital Airport**'s Terminal Three; there are usually some English speakers there who can help with the paperwork. Note that this license is only valid for driving in Beijing, and not always for rental cars, so check with rental agencies first. Beijing has heavy traffic and excellent public transportation, and hiring a local car with a driver is easy and cheap.

Weather

Temperate weather makes both spring and autumn the ideal seasons to visit the city. During summer temperatures range from 80° F (27° C) to a soaring 105° F (41° C), while winter can be anywhere from 26° F (-3° C) to 16° F (-9° C). Beijing generally has a dry climate, but summer sees frequent rain as well as some hailstorms, while winter tends to have the heaviest pollution.

Travelers with Special Needs

Since hosting the 2008 Olympics, Beijing has increased the number of barrier-free facilities. These include most attractions (and parts of the Great Wall), subways, and many buses; there are also wheelchair-friendly taxis available to order. Most shop and hotel entrances will have ramps, and most hotels have lifts.

Tourist Information

There are tourist offices in each airport terminal and around the city.

Trips and Tours

Travel China Guide, **China Highlights**, and **Discover Beijing Tours** offer standard packages and day trips. Or try **Bespoke Travel Company**'s customized tours. **Private car and van drivers** can make budget trips to the Great Wall.

Smoking and Etiquette

Smoking is banned in indoor public spaces. The legal age for drinking and smoking is 18 but rarely enforced. Be warned: cheap alcohol is usually fake and often hazardous.

Shopping

The famed fake-goods open markets are disappearing; now Beijing boasts foreign brands from Apple to Zara. Also mushrooming are chic boutiques, particularly in the areas of Gulou and Sanlitun *(see p89)*, which has the **Taikoo Li** outdoor mall and some of the city's best shops and restaurants. Other good shopping areas include Wangfujing *(see pp70–71)* in the city center and Parkview Green *(see p92)* in Chaoyang district. If you can't go without haggling, visit Panjiayuan Market for antiques, and the Silk Market for bags *(see p61)*. Traditional craft shops are best found in Gulou, and you can't beat Nan Luogu Xiang *(see p81)* for quirky souvenirs. Buy art supplies at Liulichang *(see p75)*, and reading material at **The Bookworm** in Sanlitun or the **Wangfujing Foreign Language Bookstore**.

Foreign visitors can get VAT rebates on purchases worth more than ¥500 (spent in a single store on a single day) on a stay of less than 90 days; show your passport and your receipt, and take the gifts with you on the plane.

Where to Eat

The complexity of China's eight major cuisines (and thousands of subsets) is staggering. Guangdong is famous for its dim sum and chicken's feet. Sichuan and Hunan are the spiciest cuisines, but Sichuan uses more oil and peppercorns. Landlocked Anhui stews mountain herbs and vegetables; Fujian, Jiangsu, and Zhejiang focus on seafood. The most foreign-friendly cuisine is Yunnan.

Most restaurants have a vast array of vegetables and tofu dishes, but there are also many dedicated vegetarian restaurants. Rice comes at the meal's end; avoid sticking your chopsticks in the bowl, since it resembles the incense used for funerals.

Most menus have glossy photos, if not English translations. It's a good idea to learn a few key food phrases ("something with beef/chicken," or "something spicy") and let the kitchen surprise you.

Chinese people eat together. Meals are social affairs and the host pays the check. Tipping is not expected – and often the service reflects that.

Where to Stay

For short stays, pick traditional and charming parts of the city; most hostels and courtyard hotels are located in *hutongs*, which provide food, entertainment, and hours of people-watching. They may also have cafés or rooftop bars, and even hostels can help you arrange tours or drivers. Business hotels are scattered around the city, especially in Chaoyang and the CBD. You can expect good service and excellent English, plus restaurants, a pool, a gym, and a complimentary fruit platter in the room.

DIRECTORY

PRESS
CCTV9
w english.cctv.com

China Daily
w chinadaily.com.cn

City Weekend
w cityweekend.com.cn

CRI (China Radio International)
w cri.cn

Global Times
w globaltimes.cn

That's Beijing
w thatsmags.com/beijing

Time Out Beijing
w timeoutbeijing.com

Xinhua
w xinhuanet.com

DRIVER'S LICENSE
Beijing Capital Airport
w en.bcia.com.cn

TRIPS AND TOURS
Bespoke Travel Company
(6400 0133
w bespoketravel
company.com

China Highlights
(773 283 1999
w chinahighlights.com

Discover Beijing Tours
(135 2206 9857
w discoverbeijing
tours.com

Private Car and Van Drivers
Mr. Ding
(139 1072 8962

Mr. Jack
(136 5137 4172
Mr. Li
(136 2112 7407

Travel China Guide
(29 8523 6688
w travelchinaguide.com

SHOPPING
The Bookworm
(6503 2050
w beijingbookworm.com

Taikoo Li
(6417 6110
w taikoolisanlitun.com

Wangfujing Foreign Language Bookstore
235 Wangfujing St, Dongcheng
(6512 6911

Places to Stay

> **PRICE CATEGORIES**
> Prices are based on a double room per night (with breakfast if included), with taxes and extra charges.
>
> ¥ under ¥400, ¥¥ ¥400–¥1,400, ¥¥¥ over ¥1,400

Luxury and Boutique Hotels

Brickyard
MAP H5 ■ Beigou Village, near Mutianyu, Great Wall, Huairou ■ 6162 6506 ■ brickyard atmutianyu.com ■ ¥¥
Beijing expats' first choice for romantic getaways, girls' weekends, and even weddings, the Brickyard features some impressive floor-to-ceiling windows, utterly breathtaking views, and beautiful gardens. Enjoy excellent meals made from locally sourced ingredients, and bring your swimsuit to take full advantage of the popular outdoor Jacuzzi.

Hotel Côte Cour
MAP F3 ■ 70 Yanyue Hutong ■ 6523 9598 ■ Subway: Dongsi ■ www.hotelcotecourbj.com ■ ¥¥
Hidden away amid a maze of local *hutongs*, this comfortable boutique hotel presents a modern take on a traditional *siheyuan* courtyard house. It has stylish fittings and underfloor heating that is very welcome in winter.

New World Beijing
MAP F5 ■ 8 Qinian Jie ■ 5960 8888 ■ Subway: Chongwenmen ■ beijing.newworldhotels.com ■ ¥¥
Well-located between the Temple of Heaven and Wangfujing, this hotel offers comfortable and smart rooms, a Jacuzzi and a swimming pool. It also has two Chinese restaurants and a tearoom, but its highlight is a rooftop bar.

NUO Hotel
MAP H6 ■ 2 Jiangtai Road, Chaoyang District ■ 5926 8888 ■ www.nuohotel.com ■ ¥¥
China's groundbreaking foray into the luxury market, NUO is the first of a planned 15 hotels in various global capitals. Contemporary art superstar Zeng Fanzhi, who served as consultant, installed his own original art, building a theme for the hotel's 798 Art District location.

Red Wall Garden Hotel
MAP N3 ■ 41 Shijia Hutong, Dongcheng District ■ 5169 2222 ■ www.redwallgarden hotel.com ■ ¥¥
Sometimes one must sacrifice comfort for tradition. Not so with Red Wall Garden, a luxury boutique hotel that gives you all the romance of the traditional Beijing *hutongs* and their pretty courtyards without the hard mattresses, and with soundproofed rooms.

Shadow Art Puppet Hotel
MAP D2 ■ 24 Songshu Street, Xicheng District ■ 8328 7847 ■ www.shadowartboutique.com ■ ¥¥
If your problem with other hotels is that they lack local shadow-puppet performances, look no farther. In addition to three weekly puppet shows, this courtyard hotel in historic Shichaihai also offers some free calligraphy and dumpling-making classes, plus free access to bikes. Hou Hai is only minutes away.

Aman at the Summer Palace
MAP G6 ■ 1 Gong Men Qian Jie ■ 5987 9999 ■ www.amanresorts.com ■ ¥¥¥
Guests at this stunning hotel 6 miles (10 km) northwest of the city center enjoy private access to the Summer Palace (see pp28–9), as well as a cinema, stylish spa, and subterranean swimming pool.

China World Summit Wing
MAP H4 ■ 1 Jianguo Men Wai Dajie ■ 6505 2299 ■ Subway: Guomao ■ www.shangri-la.com/beijing ■ ¥¥¥
This hotel in Beijing's tallest tower affords stunning city views from its swish Atmosphere bar on the 80th floor. There are also four restaurants, a spa, and an infinity pool.

Eclat Beijing
MAP H3 ■ 9 Dongdaqiao Lu, Chaoyang District ■ 8561 2888 ■ www.eclat hotels.com/beijing ■ ¥¥¥
A stylishly designed hotel with an impressive art collection in the public spaces, Eclat Beijing also has the capital's first pool suites. It offers a 24-hour food lounge, plus other facilities such as a personal butler service.

The Opposite House

MAP H2 ■ 11 Sanlitun Road ■ 6417 6688 ■ Subway: Tuanjiehu ■ www.theopposite house.com ■ ¥¥¥
Designed by renowned Japanese architect Kengo Kuma, The Opposite House is part of Taikoo Li Sanlitun. The 99 spacious rooms, all with natural wooden floors and deep oak soaking tubs, are a design experience, as is the stainless-steel pool.

Park Hyatt Beijing

MAP H4 ■ 2 Jianguo Men Dajie ■ 8567 1234 ■ Subway: Guomao ■ www.beijing.park. hyatt.com ■ ¥¥¥
High-end service and style are the watchwords at the Park Hyatt hotel. Chic, contemporary accommodations, coupled with stylish bars and restaurants, draw the most discerning of local and international clients.

The Peninsula Beijing

MAP N4 ■ 8 Jinyu Hutong ■ 8516 2888 ■ Subway: Dengshikou ■ www. peninsula.com ■ ¥¥¥
Luxurious rooms have plasma TVs; even the marble bathrooms also have a small screen. Two terrific restaurants (Huang Ting and Jing), a recent renovation, truly excellent service, and a central location make this one of the city's best accommodation choices.

Waldorf

MAP N4 ■ 5-15 Jinyu Hutong, off Wangfujing Street, Dongcheng District ■ 8520 8989 ■ www.waldorfastoria3. hilton.com ■ ¥¥¥
This is the jewel of downtown Beijing. Guests rave about the creative design, contemporary art display, prime location, and excellent service. For a more authentic China experience, book the ultraluxurious Hutong Villa, complete with a private swimming pool.

Courtyard Hotels

Red Lantern House

MAP D2 ■ 5 Zheng Jue Hutong, Xinjiekou Nan Dajie, Xicheng ■ 8328 5771 ■ Subway: Jishuitan ■ www.redlanternhouse. com ■ ¥
The family-owned Red Lantern House occupies a main building and two pretty courtyards. It is only a stone's throw away from the lively bars of Hou Hai.

Bamboo Garden Hotel

MAP E1 ■ 24 Xiao Shi Qiao Hutong ■ 5852 0088 ■ Subway: Gulou Dajie ■ www.bbgh.com.cn ■ ¥¥
Close to Hou Hai lake, this is the oldest of Beijing's traditional hotels, with the largest and probably most elaborate courtyards, plus beautiful rockeries and covered bridges.

Courtyard 7

MAP E2 ■ 7 Qiangulouyuan Hutong, Nan Luogu Xiang ■ 6406 0777 ■ Subway: Shichahai ■ www. courtyard7.com ■ ¥¥
This small, tastefully decorated courtyard hotel is more than 300 years old. Set back from an interesting *hutong*, it makes for a peaceful refuge. Staff are lovely and the rooms and bathrooms have been modernized beautifully.

Duge Courtyard Hotel

MAP E2 ■ 26 Qianyuanensi Hutong, Nan Luogu Xiang ■ 6445 7463 ■ Subway: Anding Men ■ www.duge courtyard.com ■ ¥¥
The Duge Courtyard's 10 individually decorated suites are designed in a dramatic and decadent fashion, and hidden away behind two imposing doors. The Peony Pavilion room is pretty and classic, while other rooms have a more contemporary vibe. All are centered on one of several small courtyards.

Kelly's Courtyard

MAP C3 ■ 25 Xiaoyuan Hutong, off Bingmasi Hutong, Xisi South Street ■ 6611 8515 ■ Subway: Xisi ■ Bus: 47, 105, 690, or 808 ■ www.kellyscourtyard. com ■ ¥¥
A stylish hideaway in a historic *hutong* near Xidan and the financial district, this hostel is owned by a travel-loving Chinese fashion designer.

The Orchid

MAP E2 ■ 65 Baochao Hutong, Dongcheng District ■ 8404 4818 ■ ¥¥
Tucked away down a quiet *hutong* in the hippest, chicest part of Beijing's Old City, The Orchid features whitewashed, airy rooms with polished hardwood floors, plus an excellent breakfast. The atmospheric terrace restaurant offers a range of Chinese, South Asian, as well as Middle Eastern meals, and they serve sundowners all day long.

Sitting On City Walls

MAP L1 ■ 57 Nianzi
Hutong, Jingshan Houjie,
near Di'an Men Nai Dajie,
Dongcheng District
■ 6402 7805 ■ Subway:
Nanluoguxiang ■ www.
beijingcitywalls.com ■ ¥¥
Beijing's best budget
courtyard and *hutong*
experience, this cozy hotel
offers free bicycle rental,
a prime location, and
plenty of local history. The
friendly, English-speaking
staff provide services
such as booking tickets,
and arranging transport
to and from the airport.

Business Hotels

East
22 Jiuxianqiao Rd,
Chaoyang ■ 8426 0888
■ www.east-beijing.com
■ ¥¥
Set amid parkland in the
INDIGO business district,
this contemporary hotel
caters to the high-end
business traveler. All 369
rooms and 23 executive
suites have amenities
such as an iPod touch,
LCD TV, free Wi-Fi, and
iHome audio system.
The hotel also has two
good restaurants, a
swimming pool, and
gym facilities.

Hilton Beijing Wangfujing
MAP M4 ■ 8 Wangfujing
Dong Dajie ■ 5812 8888
■ Subway: Wangfujing
■ www.hilton.com ■ ¥¥
Spacious, open-plan
rooms, warm service,
and a large swimming
pool are just some of
the draws at this hotel.
A central location within
walking distance of
Tian'an Men Square
and the Forbidden City
is another key feature.
Langham Place

MAP H5 ■ 1 Er Jing Rd,
opposite Terminal 3
■ 6457 5555 ■ Subway:
Beijing International
Airport ■ www.langham
hotels.com ■ ¥¥
Located near Beijing
Capital Airport, this
hotel offers luxury
rooms and suites, as
well as several modern
restaurants and bars, a
club lounge, gym, free
Wi-Fi, an art gallery,
and a free airport
shuttle bus service.

Park Plaza Hotel
MAP N3 ■ 97 Jinbao Jie
■ 8522 1999 ■ Subway:
Wangfujing ■ www.
parkplaza.com/
beijingcn ■ ¥¥
The stylish Park Plaza
is a peaceful oasis in one
of the city's fastest-devel-
oping precincts. Guest
rooms feature stylish
designer touches, and
the hotel is conveniently
located for both the
Forbidden City and
Wangfujing Dajie.

Four Seasons Beijing
MAP H1 ■ 48 Liang Ma
Qiao Lu ■ 5695 8888
■ www.fourseasons.com/
beijing ■ ¥¥¥
Exemplary service and
premium amenities await
business and leisure
travelers who stay at this
impressive modern hotel.
The interiors are artistic,
and the hotel also has two
signature restaurants, a
deluxe spa, and a popular
lounge bar.

Kerry Center Hotel
MAP H4 ■ 1 Guanghua Lu
■ 6561 8833 ■ Subway:
Guomao ■ www.shangri-
la.com ■ ¥¥¥
The Kerry Center Hotel
combines the Shangri-La
group's high service
standards with bright,
modern room design.
The Kerry is also home
to the Centro cocktail bar
(see p59) and extensive
health facilities.

The Ritz-Carlton, Beijing
MAP H6 ■ 83A Jianguo
Lu, China Central Place,
Chaoyang District
■ 5908 8888 ■ Subway:
Dawanglu ■ www.
ritzcarlton.com ■ ¥¥¥
A perfect retreat for both
business and leisure
travelers, this 305-room
deluxe hotel offers fine
dining, excellent facilities
for meetings and events,
and a high-end spa.

The Westin Beijing Chaoyang
MAP H1 ■ Bei San Huan
Dajie ■ 5922 8888
■ Subway: Liangma Qiao
■ www.starwoodhotels.
com ■ ¥¥¥
Outstanding service is
complemented by stylish
decor here. Being set on
a ring road is not ideal,
but the main sights and
shopping areas are only
a short taxi ride away.

Mid-Range Hotels

Red Hotel
MAP G2 ■ 10 Taiping
Zhuang Chunxiu Lu
■ 6417 1066 ■ Subway:
Dong Zhi Men ■ www.
red-hotel.com ■ ¥
Staying true to its name,
the former Red House Hotel
stands out with its vibrant
facade. This establishment
offers clean, cheerful
rooms, which are good
value for money. There's a
popular soccer bar on the
premises, and it's a short
walk to more bars in the
Sanlitun District.
Crystal Orange

MAP G4 ■ 25 Yonganli Zhong Jie, Chaoyang ■ 6566 1515 ■ Subway: Yonganli ■ ¥¥
This good-value hotel is furnished in bold colors, with modern paintings and Marilyn Monroe portraits adorning the walls. Comfortable rooms have spacious bathrooms and feature all modern conveniences, including Wi-Fi and iPod docks.

Hade Men Hotel
MAP N6 ■ 2A Chongwen Men Wai Dajie ■ 6711 2244 ■ Subway: Chongwen Men ■ ¥¥
The Hade Men is among the older hotels in Beijing, but it's been renovated to a good standard for this price range. Rooms are comfortable, if a bit gaudy, with pleasant views from the upper floors. It is around the corner from the railway station.

Holiday Inn Express Dong Zhi Men
MAP G2 ■ 1 Chunxiu Lu, Dongcheng ■ 6416 9999 ■ Subway: Dong Zhi Men ■ www.hiexpress.com ■ ¥¥
Centrally located between Dong Zhi Men and Gongti Bei Lu, with easy access to the city's main attractions, this hotel offers rooms at affordable prices. A good breakfast is included in the room rate, as is Wi-Fi.

Motel 268
MAP N4 ■ 19 Jin Yu Hutong ■ 5167 1666 ■ Subway: Dengshikou ■ ¥¥
Because of its prime location, this branch of China's economy hotel chain Motel 168 has been branded Motel 268. The 156-room property offers four categories of rooms, all with Internet access, air-conditioning, and TV. Be sure to ask for a room with a window.

Penta Beijing
MAP F5 ■ 3–18 Chongwen Men Wai Daije, Dongcheng ■ 6708 1188 ■ Subway: Beijing Railway Station ■ www.pentahotels.com ■ ¥¥
Located close to Tian'an Men Square and the Temple of Heaven, this stylish hotel is suited to those traveling for business and leisure. As well as good and modern in-room facilities, it offers a lounge, gym, games area, and free Wi-Fi.

Budget Hotels

Downtown Backpackers
MAP E2 ■ 85 Nan Luo Gu Xiang ■ 8400 2429 ■ Subway: Nan Luogu Xiang ■ www.backpackingchina.com ■ ¥
A good-value option in the heart of one of Beijing's most vibrant *hutongs*. This hostel is also minutes from the lakes as well as myriad restaurants and bars. It offers clean single rooms, doubles with attached bath, and 6–8 bed dorms.

Leo Hostel
MAP L6 ■ 52 Dazhalan Xijie ■ 6303 1595 ■ Subway: Qian Men ■ www.leo hostel.com ■ ¥
Leo Hostel benefits from an excellent location south of Tian'an Men Square, in among old lanes. Rooms range from 12-bed dorms to doubles; facilities range from bicycle hire to a second-hand book exchange.

Saga International Youth Hostel
MAP N3 ■ 9 Shijia Hutong ■ 6527 2773 ■ Subway: Dengshikou ■ www.saga youthhostelbeijing.cn ■ ¥
Featuring spotless doubles, triples, and dorm rooms, plus a communal kitchen and café and a rooftop patio, this hostel has helpful English-speaking staff who will organize ticket bookings and tours.

Templeside Deluxe Hutong House Hostel
MAP C3 ■ 2 Baita Xiang, Zhao Deng Yu Lu ■ 6617 2571 ■ Subway: Fucheng Men ■ www.templeside.com ■ ¥
This courtyard hostel gives budget travelers a glimpse of traditional Beijing life. It has spacious single, double, and bunk bedrooms, and a pleasant courtyard garden. Breakfast is served upon request.

The Peking International Youth Hostel
MAP E2 ■ 113-2 Nan Luogu Xiang, Dongcheng District ■ 6401 3961/ 8403 9098 ■ ¥¥
Owned by a local flower designer, this popular hostel boasts cheerful decor and an outdoor courtyard – the latter, a rare budget treat. The restaurant, while comparatively pricey, rates high, and helpful staff will arrange show tickets and day trips for you. The bustling local neighborhood is a favorite with Beijingers.

Index

Page numbers in **bold** refer to main entries.

Acknowledgments

Author
Andrew Humphreys is a travel journalist and writer who spent six months in China launching Time Out Beijing. It is his opinion that Beijing is one of the best cities in the world for food.

Publishing Director Georgina Dee

Publisher Vivien Antwi

Design Director Phil Ormerod

Editorial Ankita Awasthi Tröger, Rachel Fox, Maresa Manara, Sands Publishing Solutions, Anuroop Sanwalia, Sally Schafer, Penny Walker

Design Hansa Babra, Tessa Bindloss, Sunita Gahir, Rahul Kumar

Cover Design Richard Czapnik

Commissioned Photography Chen Chao

Picture Research Taiyaba Khatoon, Sumita Khatwani, Ellen Root

Cartography Zafar ul Islam Khan, Suresh Kumar, James MacDonald, Casper Morris

DTP Jason Little

Production Igrain Roberts

Factchecker David Leffman

Proofreader Kathryn Glendenning

Indexer Helen Peters

Picture Credits
The publisher would like to thank the following for their kind permission to reproduce their photographs:

Key: a-above; b-below/bottom; c-centre; f-far; l-left; r-right; t-top

123RF.com: Brian Kinney 4t, 16-7.

4Corners: Günter Gräfenhain 4cra; HP Huber 17cr; SIME / Tull & Bruno Morandi 35bl.

Alamy Stock Photo: age fotostock 14cla, 30br; avadaRM 17crb; Sergio Azenha 53cl; Mathias Beinling 72b; Blue Jean Images 49cr, 52tl; Jon Bower China 11bl; Robert Burch 89tl; China Images 27bl; China Photos 97cl; dpa picture alliance 30cl, 104tl; EPA 18cl; epa european pressphoto agency b.v. 46cl, 65br; Dmitry Erokhin 69tr; F1online digitale Bildagentur GmbH 96c; Wayne Farrell 64c; Kevin Foy 90cl; Victor Fraile 44cl; Jan Fritz 29tl; David Gee 15tc; Manfred Gottschalk 62c; 70cla; Tim Graham 33tr; Hemis 53tr, 90-1; Henry Westheim Photography 4clb, 33bl; jeremy sutton-hibbert 105tl; Kate Hockenhull 83tl; Iconotec 91cl; imageBROKER 71cl, 104br; jejim120 12br; JLImages 65clb; John Warburton-Lee Photography 26cla, 105cr; Patric Jonsson 82b; Michael Kemp 25cc; kpzfoto 81br; Keith Levit 61b; Sean Pavone 2tl, 3tl, 8-9, 66-7, 86-7; Wiliam Perry 76tr; Prisma Bildagentur AG 82c; Dirk Renckhoff 11tc, 54cl; REUTERS 64t, 75br; robertharding 41crb, 46b; RosalreneBetancourt 10 73cl; Hans-Joachim Schneider 39tr; Felix Stensson 99br; Keren Su / China Span 34clb; SuperStock 92cla; Ulana Switucha 27tl; TAO Images Limited 32cl, 41bl, 52c, 94tl, 100t; Lucas Vallecillos 25tc; Steve Vidler 12cl, 15cl, 60tl; View Stock 51br; Viewstock 41t; John Woods 11cl; Xinhua 51cl; Yadid Levy 1; ZUMA Press; Inc. 32-3.

AWL Images: Christian Kober 3tr, 106-7; Travel Pix Collection 28bl.

Cai Yi Xuan: Ken Seet 57bl.

Capital M Beijing: 79b.

Captial Spirits Bar: 84tl.

Courtesy Ullens Center for Contemporary Art: 31cr.

Dreamstime.com: 06photo 10ca; Aakahunaa 42c; Kyle Allen 13tl; Leonid Andronov 13br, 80ca; Aprescindere 59cla; Beijing Hetuchuangyi Images Co. Ltd. 46tc; Bertrandb 68cIb; Caoerlei 34-5; Chinaview 54tr; Chucky 78c; Chuyu 95br; Dk88888 10crb; 63br; Elena Elisseeva 58c; Julie Feinstein 58bl; Fotokon 21tl, 57tr; Frenta 98c; Igor Groshev 35cr; Horizon0428 30-1; Hungchungchih 7tr; Icara 11cra; Attila Jandi 74cl; Mike K 63tl; Klodien 102tl; Leonidfeng 70b; Yong hian Lim 76b; Linqong 45tr; Luoxubin 45bl; Mengtianhan 2tr, 36-7; Miragik 55cl; Sean Pavone 4b,18-9; William Perry 99tl; Ppy2010ha 54bl; Qin0377 10cl; Mario Savoia 55br; Yanhui Song 95t; Libo Tang 50t; Telnyawka 21cr; Winghoong Thong 4cla; Tiffanychan 44t; Vincentstthomas 21br; Vitalyedush 7bl, 10bl, 19br, 20-1, 42tl; Zheng Xiaoqiao 103br; Yuri Yavnik 103t; Xi Zhang 4cl, 75tl, 89b; Zhaohui 52b; Zhiwei Zhou 22-3; Vladimir Zhuravlev 10cr; Zjm7100 27cr, 48tl, 61tl, 68tl, 101cl.

The Georg: 56clb.

Getty Images: Getty Images: AFP 49tl, / Stephen Shaver 14b, / STR 64br; AGF 24bl; China Photos 48b; De Agostini / W. Buss 28-9; DEA Picture Library 38b; DuKai photographer 88tl; Manfred Gottschalk 78tl; Hulton Fine Art Collection 38tc; Gamma-Keystone 39cl; Christian Kober 100clb; Keith Levit 50bl; Luis Castaneda Inc. 4crb, 16bl, 96t; Tuul and Bruno Morandi 75tr; MyLoupe 20clb; Paris Match Archive 15br; Sino Images 29cr; Paul Souders 40clb; Travelasia 43b, 61cr.

iStockphoto.com: aphotostory 12-3, 62b;

bpperry 81tr; fotoVoyager 6cl; rabbit75_ist 25clb; VitalyEdush 18br; willcao911 43tl; zhaojiankang 24-5.

Janes and Hooch: Ben McMillan 58t.

Jianghu Bar: 59br.

Mosto: 56t.

Mesh Restaurant: 59clb.

Robert Harding Picture Library: Directphoto 26-7.

SuperStock: Dirk Renckhoff / imageBROKER 47tl.

The Taco Bar: 93c.

Cover

Front and spine: **4Corners:** Luigi Vaccarella.
Back: **Dreamstime.com:** Sepavo.

Pull Out Map Cover

4Corners: Luigi Vaccarella.

All other images © Dorling Kindersley
For further information see:
www.dkimages.com

Penguin
Random
House

Printed and bound in Malaysia

First published in Great Britain in 2007
by Dorling Kindersley Limited
80 Strand, London WC2R 0RL

Copyright 2007, 2017 © Dorling
Kindersley Limited

A Penguin Random House Company

17 18 19 20 10 9 8 7 6 5 4 3 2 1

Reprinted with revisions 2009, 2011, 2013, 2015, 2017

A CIP catalogue record is available from the British Library.

ISBN 978 0 2412 7899 4

MIX
Paper from
responsible sources
FSC™ C018179
www.fsc.org

SPECIAL EDITIONS OF DK TRAVEL GUIDES

DK Travel Guides can be purchased in bulk quantities at discounted prices for use in promotions or as premiums. We are also able to offer special editions and personalized jackets, corporate imprints, and excerpts from all of our books, tailored specifically to meet your own needs.

To find out more, please contact:

in the US
specialsales@dk.com

in the UK
travelguides@uk.dk.com

in Canada
specialmarkets@dk.com

in Australia
**penguincorporatesales@
penguinrandomhouse.com.au**

As a guide to abbreviations in visitor information blocks: **Adm** = admission charge; **DA** = disabled access; **D** = dinner; **L** = lunch.

Phrase Book

The Chinese language belongs to the Sino-Tibetan family of languages and uses characters which are ideographic – a symbol is used to represent an idea or an object. Mandarin Chinese, known as Putonghua in mainland China, is fairly straightforward as each character is monosyllabic. Traditionally, Chinese is written in vertical columns from top right to bottom left, however the Western style is widely used. There are several Romanization systems; the Pinyin system used here is the official system in mainland China. This phrase book gives the English word or phrase, followed by the Chinese script, then the Pinyin.

Guidelines

Pronounce vowels as in these English words:

a = as in "father"
e = as in "lurch"
i = as in "see"
o = as in "solid"
u = as in "pooh"
ü = the French u or German ü (place your lips to say "oo" and try to say "ee")

Letter combinations

Most of the consonants are pronounced as in English. As a rough guide, pronounce the following consonants as in these English words:

c = as in "hats"
q = as ch in "cheat"
x = as sh in "sheet"
z = as ds in "heads"
zh = as j in "Joe"

Mandarin Chinese is a tonal language with four tones, represented in Pinyin by one of the following marks above each vowel – the symbol shows whether the tone is flat, rising, falling and rising, or falling. The Chinese characters do not convey this information: tones are learnt when the character is learnt. Teaching tones is beyond the scope of this small phrase book, but a language course book with a CD or app will help those who wish to take the language farther.

Dialects

There are many Chinese dialects in use. It is hard to guess exactly how many, but they can be roughly classified into one of seven large groups (Mandarin, Cantonese, Hakka, Hui, etc.), each group containing a large number of more minor dialects. Although all these dialects are quite different – Cantonese uses six tones instead of four – Mandarin or Putonghua, which is mainly based on the Beijing dialect, is the official language. Despite these differences all Chinese people are more or less able to use the same formal written language so they can understand each other's writing, if not each other's speech.

In an Emergency

Help!	请帮忙！	*Qing bangmang*
Stop!	停住！	*Ting zhu*
Call a doctor!	叫医生！	*Jiao yisheng*
Call an ambulance!	叫救护车！	*Jiao jiuhuche*
Call the police!	叫警察！	*Jiao jiingcha*
Fire!	火！	*Huo*
Where is the hospital/police station?	医院/警察分局在哪里？	*Yiyuan/jingcha fenju zai nali？*

Communication Essentials

Hello	你好	*Nihao*
Goodbye	再见	*Zaijian*
Yes/No	是 / 不是	*Shi/Bushi*
... not ...	不是	*bushi*
I'm from...	我是 ... 人	*Wo shi ... ren*
I understand	我明白	*Wo mingbai*
I don't know	我不知道	*Wo bu zhidao*
Thank you	谢谢你	*Xiexie ni*
Thank you very much	多谢	*Duo xie*
Thanks (casual)	谢谢	*Xiexie*
You're welcome	不用谢	*Bu yong xie*
No, thank you	不, 谢谢你	*Bu, xiexie ni*
Please (offering)	请	*Qing*
Please (asking)	请问	*Qing wen*
I don't understand	我不明白	*Wo Bu mingbai*
Sorry/Excuse me!	抱歉 / 对不起	*Baoqian/ Duibuqi*
Could you help me please? (not emergency)	你能帮助 我吗?	*Ni neng bang zhu wo ma?*

Useful Phrases

My name is	我叫 ...	*Wo jiao ...*
Goodbye	再见	*Zaijian*
What is (this)?	(这) 是什么?	*(zhe) shi shenme?*
Could I possibly have ...? (very polite)	能不能请你 给我 ...?	*Neng buneng qing ni gei wo ...?*
Is there ... here?	这儿有 ... 吗?	*Zhe'r you ... ma?*
Where can I get ...?	我在哪里可以 得到 ...?	*Wo zai na li keyi de dao ...?*
How much is it?	它要多少钱?	*Ta yao duoshao qian?*
What time is ...?	... 什么时间?	*... shenme shijian?*
Cheers! (toast)	干杯	*Ganbei!*
Where is the restroom/toilet?	卫生间 / 洗手间在哪里?	*Weishengjian/ Xishoujian zai nali*

Signs

open	开	*kai*
closed	关	*guan*
entrance	入口	*renkou*
exit	出口	*chukou*
danger	危险	*weixian*
emergency exit	安全门	*anquanmen*
information	信息	*xinxi*
restroom	卫生间 /	*Weishengjian/*
toilet	洗手间	*Xishoujian*
men	男士	*nanshi*
women	女士	*nüshi*

Money

bank	银行	*yinhang*
cash	现金	*xianjin*
credit card	信用卡	*xinyongka*
currency exchange office	外汇兑换处	*waihui duihuanchu*
dollars	美元	*meiyuan*
pounds	英镑	*yingbang*
yuan	元	*yuan*